SCOTUS 2019

David Klein · Morgan Marietta
Editors

SCOTUS 2019

Major Decisions and Developments
of the US Supreme Court

Editors
David Klein
Department of Political Science
Eastern Michigan University
Ypsilanti, MI, USA

Morgan Marietta
Department of Political Science
University of Massachusetts Lowell
Lowell, MA, USA

ISBN 978-3-030-29955-2   ISBN 978-3-030-29956-9   (eBook)
https://doi.org/10.1007/978-3-030-29956-9

Cover design by Oscar Spigolon and eStudio Calamar

This Palgrave Macmillan imprint is published by the registered company Springer Nature Switzerland AG
The registered company address is: Gewerbestrasse 11, 6330 Cham, Switzerland

Contents

Notes on Contributors

Lawrence Baum is Professor Emeritus of Political Science at Ohio State University. The primary focus of his research is the explanation of judges' choices as decision makers. His most recent books are *Ideology on the Supreme Court* (Princeton University Press, 2017), *The Battle for the Court: Interest Groups, Judicial Elections, and Public Policy* (University of Virginia Press, 2017, with co-authors David Klein and Matthew Streb), *The Company They Keep: How Partisan Divisions Came to the Supreme Court* (Oxford University Press, 2019, with co-author Neal Devins), and *The Supreme Court*, 13th edition (CQ Press, 2019).

Bethany Blackstone is Associate Professor of Political Science at the University of North Texas. Her research interests focus on American political institutions with particular emphasis on interbranch relations, judicial politics, and legislative politics. Her current research focuses on reconsideration of precedent in the US courts of appeals and the role of the US Supreme Court in contemporary American policymaking. Her previous work has been published in a number of journals including *The Journal of Politics, Law & Society Review, PS: Political Science & Politics, Justice System Journal*, and *Research and Politics*.

Jennifer Bowie is Associate Professor of Political Science at the University of Richmond in Richmond, Virginia. She is currently the Editor of the *Law and Politics Book Review* and is the author of *The View from the Bench and Chambers: Examining Judicial Process and Decision Making on the U.S. Courts of Appeals* (University of Virginia Press, 2014 with Donald R. Songer and John Szmer). Her research has appeared in a number of journals including *The Journal of Politics, Political Research Quarterly, The Journal of Law and Courts,* and *Justice System Journal*. Her research interests include examining judicial decision making in the US Courts of Appeals and state courts.

Pamela C. Corley is Associate Professor and Director of the Law and Legal Reasoning Minor in the Political Science Department at Southern Methodist University. Her research focuses on the US Supreme Court. She is the author of *Concurring Opinion Writing on the U.S. Supreme Court* (SUNY Press, 2010), and the co-author of *The Puzzle of Unanimity: Consensus on the United States Supreme Court* (Stanford University Press, 2013). She has published articles in *Journal of Politics, Law & Society Review, Political Research Quarterly, Judicature, Law & Policy, Journal of Legal Studies, Journal of Supreme Court History, Publius: The Journal of Federalism, Justice System Journal,* and *American Politics Research*.

Brett Curry is Professor of Political Science at Georgia Southern University. His research centers on aspects of judicial politics and decision making. His scholarship has been published in a number of journals including the *Journal of Politics, Law & Society Review, Law & Social Inquiry, American Politics Research* and *Justice System Journal*. His co-authored book, *Decision Making by the Modern Supreme Court,* was published with Cambridge University Press in 2011. A second book, *U.S. Attorneys, Political Control, and Career Ambition,* was recently published by Oxford University Press.

Gerard Michael D'Emilio is an attorney in Oklahoma City, Oklahoma. He received his J.D. with highest honors from the University of Oklahoma College of Law, graduating first in his class; his M.M. in Vocal Performance from Westminster Choir College; and his

B.M. in Voice and B.A. with highest honors in Politics from Oberlin College and Conservatory of Music. He is a former student of his co-author, Ronald Kahn, with whom he has collaborated on numerous projects. He served as a judicial law clerk for the US District Court for the Western District of Oklahoma over the 2018–2019 term, and he will again serve in that capacity for the US Court of Appeals for the Tenth Circuit over the 2020–2021 term.

Abigail Diebold is a senior at Swarthmore College and an honors candidate majoring in Political Science and History with an emphasis on American political development. She currently works for Congresswoman Mary Gay Scanlon (PA-05), and has worked as the Communications and Political Director for Rep. Jennifer O'Mara and a Communications Intern for Senator Jeff Merkley. In addition to conducting research with Professor Nackenoff, she has completed an independent research project on the political history of Delaware County and is on the editorial board of the Swarthmore *Phoenix* (Swarthmore College's only print newspaper).

Mark Graber is the Jacob A. France Professor of Constitutionalism at the University of Maryland School of Law. He is the author of *A New Introduction to American Constitutionalism* (Oxford University Press) and co-editor (with Keith Whittington and Howard Gillman) of *American Constitutionalism: Structures and Powers* and *American Constitutionalism: Rights and Powers* (both from Oxford University Press). He is presently working on *Forged in Failure*, a book that will examine how much constitutional change in the United States has been caused by the failure of constitutional practices to function as expected.

Ronald Kahn is Erwin N. Griswold Professor of Politics Emeritus, Oberlin College. He is a specialist in constitutional law, legal theory, and American political development, and the author of *The Supreme Court and Constitutional Theory, 1953–1993* (1994) and *The Supreme Court and American Political Development* (with Ken I. Kersch, 2006), both published by University Press of Kansas. His most recent book is *Constructing Individual Rights in a Conservative Age: The Supreme Court and Social Change in the Rehnquist and Roberts Court Eras* (with

Gerard D'Emilio, forthcoming, Kansas, 2020). Recent publications: "The Jurisprudence of Justice Scalia: Common Law Judging Behind an Originalist Facade," in *The Conservative Revolution of Antonin Scalia.* Ed. David A. Schultz and Howard Schweber, (Lexington Books, 2018) (with Gerard D'Emilio) and "Supreme Court Decision-making and the Social Construction Process: Continuity in a Polarized Age," 4 *Constitutional Studies* (2019), part of a Festschrift in his honor.

David Klein is Professor and Department Head at Eastern Michigan University. He served as the inaugural editor of the *Journal of Law & Courts* (2011–2017) and is the author of three books: *Making Law in the United States Courts of Appeals* (Cambridge University Press, 2002), *American Courts Explained: A Detailed Introduction to the Legal Process Using Real Cases* (West Academic Publishing 2016, with Gregory Mitchell), and *The Battle for the Court: Interest Groups, Judicial Elections, and Public Policy* (University of Virginia Press, 2017, with Lawrence Baum and Matthew Streb). With Morgan Marietta, he is co-editor of the annual *SCOTUS* series at Palgrave Macmillan on the major decisions of the Supreme Court.

Gary Lawson is the Philip S. Beck Professor at Boston University School of Law. He has authored or co-authored five books on jurisprudence, constitutional history, and constitutional law; eight editions of a textbook on federal administrative law; a forthcoming textbook on constitutional law, and more than eighty scholarly articles. He is an associate editor of *The Heritage Guide to the Constitution.* His recent books include *"A Great Power of Attorney": Understanding the Fiduciary Constitution* (University Press of Kansas, 2017) (with Guy Seidman) and *Evidence of the Law: Proving Legal Claims* (University of Chicago Press, 2017).

Rory Little is the Joseph W. Cotchett Professor of Law at U.C. Hastings College of the Law, where he has taught for 26 years. He is a graduate of Yale Law School and clerked for US Supreme Court Justices Brennan, Stevens, and Stewart—all in one year. He practiced privately and as a federal criminal lawyer for 12 years before teaching fulltime and is currently "Of Counsel" to the law firm of McDermott Will &

Emery. He teaches and lectures widely on Constitutional, Criminal Law and Procedure, and Legal Ethics topics and has published a number of scholarly works. You can find his regular commentary about the US Supreme Court's criminal docket at SCOTUSblog.com.

Morgan Marietta is Associate Professor of Political Science at the University of Massachusetts Lowell. He is the author of four books, *The Politics of Sacred Rhetoric, A Citizen's Guide to American Ideology, A Citizen's Guide to the Constitution and the Supreme Court*, and most recently *One Nation, Two Realities: Dueling Facts in American Democracy* on the causes and consequences of polarized perceptions of facts (Oxford University Press, with David Barker at American University). He and Bert Rockman from Purdue University are the co-editors of the *Citizen Guides to Politics & Public Affairs*, a series of books from Routledge dedicated to explaining the core issues and institutions of American politics. With David Klein, he is co-editor of the annual *SCOTUS* series at Palgrave Macmillan on the major decisions of the Supreme Court.

Carol Nackenoff is Richter Professor of Political Science at Swarthmore College, where she teaches constitutional law and American politics. She composed the entry on the Supreme Court for Oxford Bibliographies Online. She is the author of *The Fictional Republic: Horatio Alger and American Political Discourse* (1994) and co-editor of *Statebuilding from the Margins* (with Julie Novkov, 2014) and of *Jane Addams and the Practice of Democracy* (with Marilyn Fischer and Wendy Chmielewski, 2009). Her most recent book is *Stating the Family: New Directions in the Study of American Politics* (with Julie Novkov, forthcoming, 2020). Her current research examines conflicts over the extent and terms of incorporation of women, African Americans, Native Americans, workers, and immigrants into the polity between 1875 and 1925 and the role that organized women played in pressing new definitions of public work on the American state. She received her Ph.D. from the University of Chicago.

Stephen Simon is Associate Professor of Political Science at the University of Richmond. Before entering academia, he received a J.D. from the New York University School of Law, clerked for a federal district court judge, and practiced law for several years in a Washington, DC. law firm. Since receiving his Ph.D. in Government and Politics (from the University of Maryland), he has taught courses in constitutional law, jurisprudence, and political theory. In addition to a number of articles on civil liberties, foreign law, and the Supreme Court, he is the author of *Universal Rights and the Constitution* (SUNY Press, 2014) and *The U.S. Supreme Court and the Domestic Force of International Human Rights Law* (Lexington Books, 2016). He is currently the Coordinator of the University of Richmond's program in Philosophy, Politics, Economics, and Law (PPEL).

Marian Williams is Professor of Criminal Justice in the Department of Government and Justice Studies at Appalachian State University. Her research focuses on the court process, especially issues surrounding the bail system, the right to counsel, capital punishment, and race and gender disparities the court system. Articles on these issues can be found in a number of journals, including *Criminology, Justice Quarterly,* and *Journal of Crime and Justice.* Her research on civil asset forfeiture can be found in *Criminology and Public Policy* and *Journal of Criminal Justice.*

Many thanks to our editorial assistant **Daniel Bauman**, UMass Lowell '22.

1

Introduction: The 2018–2019 Term at the Supreme Court

Morgan Marietta

Two hundred and thirty-one years after the signing of the US Constitution in 1787, the Supreme Court addressed its meaning in four key areas during the 2018–2019 term: *defendants' rights, fair elections, separation of powers*, and the *establishment of religion*. Several major cases considered the rights of criminal defendants across a range of issues from jury selection to the death penalty. Two cases addressed election rules and the role of the Court in questions of partisan manipulation. Two cases dealt with how government agencies make influential decisions, grounded in how the Constitution divides powers among branches of the federal government. And the Court re-examined an old controversy about religious symbols in the public square. Each dispute has a strong influence on American life and law. In the following chapters, noted scholars of American law and politics discuss the major decisions of the year, concluding with a discussion of Justice Brett Kavanaugh's first year and its implications for the future of the Court.

M. Marietta (✉)
Department of Political Science, University of Massachusetts Lowell,
Lowell, MA, USA

© The Author(s) 2020
D. Klein and M. Marietta (eds.), *SCOTUS 2019*,
https://doi.org/10.1007/978-3-030-29956-9_1

To summarize the year's major rulings, they

1. Allow the death penalty to proceed (under the Eighth Amendment's prohibition of "cruel and unusual punishment") if the prisoner has a medical condition that causes excessive pain during the execution or does not remember the crime due to mental incapacitation, but *not* if a mental condition (including dementia) precludes the prisoner from understanding the reason for their execution,

2. Allow separate prosecutions by state and federal governments for the same act under the *separate sovereigns* doctrine without violating the Fifth Amendment prohibition against double jeopardy,

3. Allow law enforcement officers to draw a blood alcohol test from an unconscious driver without a warrant (which is not a violation of the Fourth Amendment's protection against "unreasonable searches and seizures"),

4. Apply the Excessive Fines Clause of the Eighth Amendment to actions by state governments (and await further proceedings to determine if civil asset forfeitures of cars or other high-value items are considered excessive),

5. Enforce the prohibition against using race to dismiss potential jurors during jury selection (a *Batson* violation, supported by the Sixth Amendment's jury right and the Fourteenth Amendment's guarantee of equal protection of the laws),

6. Prohibit additional mandatory minimum prison sentences without a jury trial (protected by the Sixth Amendment) for the commission of crimes while on supervised release following a period of incarceration,

7. Allow partisan gerrymandering—the practice of shifting the boundaries of electoral districts to advantage the party in power—as a political problem left to the representative branches rather than a question of rights determined by the judicial branch,

8. Disallow the Census Bureau from adding a citizenship question to the 2020 census without an accurate justification,

9. Continue to allow Congress to delegate policymaking authority to federal agencies without violating the separation of powers or the non-delegation doctrine,

10. Continue to defer to federal agencies to determine the meaning of terms employed in their own regulations (known as *Auer* deference),
11. Allow long-standing religious monuments to remain on public land (which is not a violation of the First Amendment's prohibition of the establishment of religion).

Criminal Law and the Rights of Defendants

Of the ten Amendments that form the Bill of Rights, four address the rights of defendants in criminal prosecutions. This emphasis reflects the Founders' concerns with a common practice of tyrannical governments: charging enemies of the regime with crimes they did not commit, in order to remove them and intimidate others. This was done by the British crown (and other European royals) in the 1700s just as it is done by the Russian government (among others) today. The same threat applies to individuals and groups that are simply not popular with the majority or with the current elected leaders. For these reasons, Amendments IV, V, VI, and VIII include a wide range of protections against false prosecution. A major theme of this year's cases is the tension between legitimate aims of law enforcement and necessary protections of individual rights against government overreach.

The Court addressed defendants' and convicts' rights regarding the death penalty, double jeopardy, blood alcohol tests, excessive fines, jury selection, and re-imprisonment during supervised release. Given the current Court's conservative majority (Justices Alito, Gorsuch, Kavanaugh, Roberts, and Thomas), we might expect a consistent set of law and order outcomes ruling in favor of government prosecutors, with the four liberal Justices (Breyer, Ginsburg, Kagan, and Sotomayor) in dissent supporting the rights of defendants. But the outcomes were much more balanced and mixed.

To start with the most extreme imposition on liberty—the death penalty—the Court upheld the constitutionality of capital punishment when its imposition may cause severe pain, because as Justice Gorsuch phrased it, "the Eighth Amendment does not guarantee a prisoner a painless death."[1] However, in a different case the Court ruled that a prisoner cannot be executed if he is unable to "rationally understand the reasons for his death sentence," which may be caused by dementia as well as forms of psychosis already recognized by the Court.[2] One outcome supported the imposition of the death penalty (5-4 divided by ideology) and the other limited it (with Chief Justice Roberts joining the four liberal Justices). In his discussion of these cases in Chapter 9, Mark Graber describes them as disputes over capital punishment at the margins, accepting the core constitutionality of the practice but not the details of its application. The debates reveal long-term disagreements among the Justices over the purposes as well as the procedures of the death penalty.

In the next two controversies, the Court upheld government prosecutions. *Gamble v. U.S.* allows for successive prosecutions by both state and federal governments (in Terance Gamble's case for the illegal possession of a firearm). In Chapter 5, Rory Little explains how seven Justices believe this practice does not violate the Double Jeopardy Clause of the Fifth Amendment. Likewise, *Mitchell v. Wisconsin* allows an unconscious motorist to be subjected to a blood alcohol test without violating the Fourth Amendment's protection against unreasonable searches and seizures. In Chapter 10, Pamela Corley explains the Court's closely divided 5-4 ruling and its potential ramifications for allowing other searches without a warrant under the exigent circumstances exception.

One of the unresolved questions of the US Constitution was whether the Eighth Amendment's protections against excessive fines create a restriction against the actions of state governments (in addition to the federal government). In Chapter 12's discussion of *Timbs v. Indiana*, Marian Williams explains how that question has been resolved, but still

---

[1] *Bucklew* decision, page 12. A brief note on citations in the volume: Recent decisions have not yet been printed in the *U.S. Reports* that collect all Supreme Court decisions at the Library of Congress (so the page number in the volume is still blank, as in 573 U.S. ___). To identify quotes from the recent decisions, we will use page numbers from the slip opinions issued immediately by the Court, which are readily available online at the U.S. Supreme Court Web site (www.supremecourt.gov/opinions). Links to opinions, oral arguments, briefs by each party, and many other details are also available at SCOTUSblog.com.

[2] *Madison* decision, page 11.

to be decided is its application to the constitutionality of *civil forfeiture*: Can a state government seize assets like cars or boats used in the commission of crimes, especially when those assets are disproportionately large?

The last two cases clearly uphold the rights of defendants and convicts. In *Flowers v. Mississippi*, the Court addressed another chapter of the long-standing controversy about the role of race in jury selection. In Chapter 4, Jennifer Bowie discusses how the *Batson* decision in 1986 outlawed the dismissal of potential jurors on the basis of race. In *Flowers*, a decisive majority upheld a claim that *Batson* had been violated in a repeated set of trials characterized by the dismissal of black jurors by the prosecutor without adequate race-neutral justifications. The Court clearly reaffirmed its commitment to the *Batson* holding, including the types of evidence defendants may use in making a *Batson* challenge.

The final criminal law case addresses the right to a jury trial during *post-conviction* proceedings. *Supervised release* is the term for the period of time after completing a prison sentence in which the government can re-invoke prison time if the convict commits a further offense. Individuals on supervised release may be re-imprisoned if a judge finds after a hearing that they have committed an offense. However, in *U.S. v. Haymond*, the Court held that the right to a jury trial applies in at least some cases of re-imprisonment. As Stephen Simon discusses in Chapter 7, Andre Haymond was subjected to a mandatory minimum sentence of five years for the commission of a crime—possession of child pornography—while on supervised release. Emphasizing that the mandatory minimum expanded the sentence beyond the time period authorized by the jury's verdict at his original conviction, a slim majority of the Court concluded that Haymond's right to a trial had been violated. The dissenters see this ruling as not only wrong under the Constitution but also creating deep practical problems for how courts handle the supervision of convicts after release. In sum, the Court's decisions this year on criminal procedures are a somewhat unexpected mix of pro-defendant and pro-prosecution rulings.

Fair Elections

Perhaps the two most politically charged cases this year were about fair elections. The census case and the gerrymandering case are intimately connected: The Constitution commands a count of the population every ten years so we can know how many representatives in Congress and votes in the Electoral College each state receives for the following decade. The same data are then used by each state to draw the new boundaries of its electoral districts (based on shifting populations in various parts of the state). *Counting* and then *drawing* are two interconnected parts of American elections. However, allegations that those processes are tainted by partisan motives are one-step removed from the individual right to vote, which is more clearly protected. These cases present questions about fair election procedures, which make constitutional violations more difficult to identify or rectify.

Department of Commerce v. New York is about whether including the question, "Is this person a citizen of the United States?" on the census form that goes to each American household violates the Constitution, or at least violates the bounds set by Congress on the behavior of executive agencies. The plaintiffs contend that the commerce secretary, Wilbur Ross, intentionally added the citizenship question to discourage recent Hispanic immigrants from filling out the census form. This would violate the constitutional command to conduct an accurate count. The challengers also argue that the *process* Ross employed to make his decision violated the normal procedures mandated by Congress, amounting to an "arbitrary and capricious" action. Ross claims that the citizenship question serves legitimate purposes and that he has the clear authority to add it to the questionnaire. Underneath this argument is the deeply polarizing debate over who gets to be represented in our system. Is it everyone living in the United States? Or is it just citizens? If "the people" are to be represented, defining those people in the current political age has proved to be deeply divisive. But it must be done if the census is to count the people who count.

In Chapter 3, Brett Curry explains the divisions among three perspectives: the four Justices who believe the question violates the

Constitution, the four who would allow it, and the narrow opinion of Chief Justice John Roberts, which turned the proceedings back to the Commerce Department to provide an accurate justification. In Roberts' decisive view, the evidence "tells a story that does not match the explanation the Secretary gave for his decision," suggesting that "what was provided here was more of a distraction."[3] The rejection by the Court led to the abandonment of the citizenship question on the 2020 census, but not future political and judicial questions about whether representation and redistricting must be based on residency or on citizenship.

While the Court considered the question about the *2020* census, it also considered two cases about the redrawing of electoral districts conducted in the wake of the *2010* census with the data from that earlier count. The gerrymandering case—*Rucho v. Common Cause*—is about whether the political party in control of a state legislature can alter the electoral maps to make it harder for their party to be removed from office (i.e., by concentrating members of the other party in one district, so several other districts predictably reelect the party in power). This kind of partisan gerrymandering was undertaken by Republicans in North Carolina and by Democrats in Maryland. To many, this sounds like a clear violation of representative democracy. But the Court may not be able to discern a right that has been violated, or to agree on a standard of evidence to know if it has been violated, or to provide a means to fix the problem. As Carol Nackenoff and Abigail Diebold describe the *Rucho* ruling in Chapter 11, a narrow majority of the Court found this to be a political question left to the electoral branches to solve rather than a matter for federal courts to settle. Perhaps the most intense dissent of the term was made by Justice Elena Kagan in expressing her "deep sadness" that "the practices challenged in these cases imperil our system of government."[4]

---

[3] *Department of Commerce* decision, pages 27, 28.
[4] *Rucho* Kagan dissent, page 33.

Separation of Powers

While the violations of rights are the focus of many constitutional questions, another set of questions address the *structures* of government which are also meant to protect individual citizens from potential abuses. One of the most prominent of these is the *separation of powers*, or the division of American government into independent and often competing institutions, each exercising only limited authority. This is meant to prevent the centralization of power, which can lead to abuse and corruption when a small number of leaders are able to impose their will without a check on their decisions. The Constitution intentionally separates the power to make laws from the power to enforce them and separates both from the power to judge their legitimacy. Those who exercise one form of power are generally forbidden from invoking another form as well. Some Justices see the separation of powers as a crucial check on government abuse of citizens, as well as a necessary device for allowing voters to know exactly who was responsible for implementing a policy. Others see these separations as less definitive and protective in an era when government fulfills many complex functions.

The debate becomes more complicated when we consider administrative agencies within the executive branch—like the Environmental Protection Agency, the Federal Election Commission, and many other agencies—which create regulations, enforce violations, and make specific decisions that Congress cannot necessarily anticipate. The growth in the range and reach of the federal bureaucracy has complicated the question of how much the principle of separation of powers should be enforced by the Court. There is a strong partisan dimension to this dispute. Political conservatives tend to oppose the expansion of the bureaucracy, while political liberals tend to advocate the increased role of federal agencies in regulation of the economy, the environment, violations of minority rights, and many other progressive goals. Both important cases this year on the separation of powers are about federal agencies—specifically the Veterans Administration (VA) and the Department of Justice (DOJ)—and whether their actions exercise legislative power they do not possess or avoid oversight the judiciary should exert.

Gundy v. U.S. is about whether the Congress unconstitutionally gave the DOJ the authority to decide which Americans would be included in the national sex offender registry. The question of *Gundy* is whether the delegation of decision-making authority to the DOJ left the Attorney General as a legitimate *enforcer* of the law or an illegitimate *creator* of law. In Chapter 6, Gary Lawson explains the deeply divided ruling that the arrangement of authority between Congress and the DOJ does not violate the non-delegation doctrine or the separation of powers. However, the divided Court that heard this case *before* the confirmation of Brett Kavanaugh may alter this view in the future with a full roster of nine Justices, moving toward Justice Gorsuch's view that "the Constitution promises that only the people's elected representatives may adopt new federal laws restricting liberty."[5]

Kisor v. Wilkie is about a different separation of powers question: whether courts should oversee the decisions of federal agencies when they determine the meaning of terms in their own regulations. Allowing agencies to make these kinds of decisions is referred to as *Auer* deference, after a 1997 Supreme Court ruling that limited judicial oversight of agency rulings unless they are clearly unreasonable.[6] As Bethany Blackstone discusses in Chapter 8, the Court has wrestled with the questions of when congressional legislation is ambiguous or clear, when agencies are being reasonable or unreasonable, and when the Court should replace the agency's judgment with its own. A closely divided Court (5–4, with Roberts joining the liberal Justices) ruled in favor of maintaining *Auer* deference, though defining it more clearly and limiting the scope of when agency decisions remain independent of judicial intervention.

Neither case announced a new rule enforcing greater separation of powers, as many conservatives wanted, but instead maintained the

---

[5] *Gundy* Gorsuch dissent, page 1.
[6] *Auer v. Robbins*, 519 U.S. 42 (1997).

status quo. However, both decisions leave room for future rulings that may take a less accommodating view of the powers of federal agencies.

Religion

To end with the first chapter of the volume (the cases are presented in alphabetical order), *American Legion v. American Humanist* presents a good-old-fashioned religious controversy. Does the imposing Bladensburg Peace Cross, maintained as a World War I memorial on public land next to a major highway, violate the Establishment Clause of the First Amendment? While the Free Exercise Clause sets limits to government interference with the right of Americans to worship as they choose, the Establishment Clause sets limits to government actions supporting religion. But what exactly are those limits? So many varying facets characterize religious displays and monuments—the timing of their creation, the different religious traditions represented, their disputed meanings—that the Court has had great trouble identifying a clear and consistent application of the Establishment Clause in this area.

Ron Kahn and Gerard D'Emilio discuss the controversy in *American Legion* and the Court's ruling which emphasizes the role of history in assessing public monuments of considerable age. Only two Justices took the view that "when a cross is displayed on public property, the government may be presumed to endorse its religious content."[7] The majority of Justices—including Breyer and Kagan—joined the decision arguing that "retaining established, religiously expressive monuments, symbols, and practices is quite different from erecting or adopting new ones. The passage of time gives rise to a strong presumption of constitutionality."[8] The majority argues that this is the case because "the Religion Clauses of the Constitution aim to foster a society in which people of all beliefs can live together harmoniously, and the presence of the Bladensburg Cross on the land where it has stood for so many years is

---

[7]*American Legion* Ginsburg dissent, page 5.
[8]*American Legion* decision, page 21.

fully consistent with that aim."[9] On the other hand, "a government that roams the land, tearing down monuments with religious symbolism and scrubbing away any reference to the divine will strike many as aggressively hostile to religion."[10]

This reading of the Religion Clauses of the First Amendment is also reflected in other recent decisions, including *Trinity Lutheran* in 2017 and *Masterpiece Cakeshop* in 2018. What connects *American Legion* and those other rulings is that in all three recent cases the claimant—a church, a business, and a veterans group—won at the Supreme Court after losing at lower courts. All three cases protected the role of religion in public life, and all three feature the same split of Justices: 7-2 with Breyer and Kagan joining the more conservative Justices (against dissents by Ginsburg and Sotomayor). The Court contains a dominant majority of Justices who take a pluralist position on religious controversies, shifting the constitutional standard toward more protection for religious expression in the public square.

Directions of the Court

Before discussing how some of the rulings this year fit together and suggest possible future directions of the Court, it is important to note a part of its past. Justice John Paul Stevens passed away in July of 2019 at the age of 99. He was one of the longest-serving Justices in the history of the Court, deciding cases from 1975 to 2010, when he was replaced by Elena Kagan. Though nominated by a Republican President (Gerald Ford), he became a leader of the liberal wing of the Court. When he joined the Court, it was populated by liberal lions William Brennan and Thurgood Marshall; by the time he retired thirty-five years later he had sworn in John Roberts as the Chief Justice and witnessed the shift to a more conservative Court.

---

[9]Ibid., page 2.
[10]Ibid., page 20.

Noted for his distinctive bow ties, he was deeply influenced by his military service in World War II and endorsed a form of constitutional protection of patriotism that surprised many. Stevens was commissioned as a Naval Officer on December 6, 1941, the day before Pearl Harbor. When the Court ruled that flag-burning was protected by the First Amendment in *Texas v. Johnson* in 1989, Stevens could not join the majority, which included not only the famously liberal Justices Brennan, Marshall, and Blackmun, but also Kennedy and Scalia. Stevens wrote that the flag has an "intangible dimension" that other free speech concerns do not, because "the value of the flag as a symbol cannot be measured." The flag, he said, transcends other constitutional concerns, because if the ideas it symbolizes "are worth fighting for—and our history demonstrates that they are—it cannot be true that the flag that uniquely symbolizes their power is not itself worthy of protection from unnecessary desecration."[11]

During his time on the bench, Stevens supported the constitutionality of affirmative action and the unconstitutionality of executing the mentally disabled. He favored abortion rights, opposed government endorsements of religion, and moved left on the death penalty. He wrote *Chevron*, upholding deference to administrative agencies, which was at issue this year in *Kisor* (and likely will be again in the future). He dissented in *Heller* on gun rights. If he were on the bench this year, he would in all likelihood have joined the dissenters in *American Legion* on religious monuments, in *Bucklew* on the death penalty, and especially in *Rucho* on gerrymandering. In a speech commemorating his 30th year on the Court, he explained that "learning on the job is essential to the process of judging," perhaps the key to his judicial evolution.[12]

---

[11] *Texas v. Johnson* 491 U.S. 397 (1989) at 436, 437, 439.
[12] 2005 speech at Fordham Law School.

Judicial Review

At the heart of constitutional controversy is the power of the Supreme Court to declare actions of the government to be null and void because they violate the Constitution. This power of judicial review is not described in the Constitution but nonetheless is thought essential to its operation and the protection of individual rights. How expansive or limited judicial review should be is a deeply controversial question, especially when it pits the judgment of the Justices against the judgment of electoral majorities. Several major cases this term revealed the disagreements among the current Justices about the legitimate role of the Court.

Perhaps the clearest example—with the strongest partisan implications—was *Rucho v. Common Cause*, in which the Court refused to exercise its powers and instead left the problem of gerrymandering to the electoral branches. In *Kisor*, the Court backed away from intervening in decisions made by federal agencies. In the death penalty cases, the Court split over whether to allow legislative majorities to determine when capital punishment is appropriate or to replace electoral judgment with judicial judgment. A major shift may be developing in how the Court deals with requests for stays of execution. Led by Justice Gorsuch, the era of leniency in granting last-minute appeals may be coming to an end, signaling repeated and emotional future conflicts given the Court's deep disagreements about the legitimacy of the death penalty and its applications. In each of these situations, the Justices divided over the proper role of the Court in solving the problems of democracy.

Precedent

One of the abiding questions the Court faces is the extent to which its earlier decisions are binding under the principle of *stare decisis*. This may be especially important in an era of ideological shift, when a new majority may want to overturn previous rulings. In *American Legion*, the Justices argued that the long-standing *Lemon* test defining the limits of government action under the Establishment Clause had not aged well and was unworkable in many contexts. In her dissent, Justice Ginsburg complains about "diminishing precedent."[13] However, her dissent in *Gamble* emphasizes that "*stare decisis* is not an inexorable command," and therefore, "I would not cling to those ill-advised decisions."[14] The truth may be that when it comes to precedent, standards are unclear and Justices seem flexible.[15] Though often invoked by those on the losing side of a decision, precedent is not a strong barrier when individual Justices see a violation of the Constitution.

The debate over precedent was taken up strenuously in *Gamble*. Like Ginsburg on the left, Gorsuch on the right was unimpressed by the power of precedent in his dissent, arguing that "*stare decisis* has many virtues, but when it comes to enforcing the Constitution this Court must take (and has always taken) special care in the doctrine's application… And while we rightly pay heed to the considered views of those who have come before us… *stare decisis* isn't supposed to be the 'art of being methodically ignorant of what everyone knows'."[16] Ironically, Justice Thomas ruled *in favor* of the precedent in *Gamble*, but nonetheless wrote a concurrence solely to make clear that this was *not* the reason for his position. He wanted to clarify for future reference that "when faced with a demonstrably wrong precedent, my rule is simple: We should not follow it."[17]

Ideological Divisions

The Court is now composed of five generally conservative and four generally liberal Justices. But the 5-4 Court did not produce dominantly conservative decisions this year. *Bucklew* upholding the imposition of

---

[13]*American Legion* Ginsburg dissent, page 2.

[14]*Gamble* Ginsburg dissent, pages 2, 7.

[15]The Justices also overruled precedents this year in *Franchise Tax Board of California v. Hyatt* and *Knick v. Township of Scott* (see Chapter 13).

[16]*Gamble* Gorsuch dissent, page 18, quoting Jeremy Bentham.

[17]*Gamble* Thomas concurrence, page 9.

the death penalty is on the conservative side, but *Madison*, limiting its application, is a liberal decision (with Roberts as the swing vote in each five-Justice majority). *Gamble* and *Mitchell* were pro-prosecutor rulings, but *Flowers* and *Haymond* ruled in favor of defendants. The fair elections rulings split, one on the conservative side (gerrymandering) and the other on the liberal side (the census citizenship question). The separation of powers cases both came down on the liberal side, while *American Legion* on the establishment of religion was a more conservative decision. So what accounts for several cases ending up with liberal rulings even though the Court is 5-4 conservative?

One answer is that Brett Kavanaugh was not yet on the Court for *Gundy*, which may well have gone the conservative direction if he had voted. The broader answer is that the conservative majority is composed of very different thinkers, and it only takes one of the five to defect for the balance to shift. Three times it was Roberts alone, on the application of the death penalty, upholding deference to the decisions of federal agencies, and in the census case. Roberts, Alito, and Kavanaugh all joined the liberal Justices on race in jury selection. It was Gorsuch who took the liberal side on the jury right in post-conviction proceedings. Gorsuch has distinguished himself from the other conservative Justices as less trustful of government actors in criminal proceedings and more concerned about the constitutional protections of double jeopardy, juries, and the vagueness of government powers that may arbitrarily trample liberties.

Chapter 13 discusses seven additional cases that may well have earned individual chapters of their own if space in this brief volume had allowed it. Several cases are about who can and cannot be sued under various conditions (states, local governments, police, companies in class-actions, and even Apple in the ongoing dispute about pricing in the App Store). Three of these cases divide 5-4 along ideological lines, while four others depend on much more interesting divisions among the Justices. The rulings of 2019 are mixed, nuanced, and often surprising.

2

American Legion v. American Humanist on Religious Monuments Under the First Amendment

Ronald Kahn and Gerard D'Emilio

Thirty years ago in *County of Allegheny v. American Civil Liberties Union*, the Supreme Court was faced with a menorah and a manger.[1] Asked to decide whether these displays violated the First Amendment's Establishment Clause, the Court split—and in doing so split the baby, holding that the manger (or crèche) violated the Establishment Clause, but that the menorah did not.[2] Some Justices found that the crèche impermissibly conveyed a governmental endorsement of Christianity, primarily because of the context in which the government displayed it. But that same context-heavy analysis also led several Justices to see the

---

[1]492 U.S. 573 (1989)

[2]U.S. Constitution, Amendment I ("Congress shall make no law respecting an establishment of religion…").

R. Kahn (✉)
Oberlin College, Oberlin, OH, USA
e-mail: rkahn@oberlin.edu

G. D'Emilio
Oklahoma City, OK, USA

© The Author(s) 2020
D. Klein and M. Marietta (eds.), *SCOTUS 2019*,
https://doi.org/10.1007/978-3-030-29956-9_2

menorah as permissible. Other Justices felt both displays were fine, as no governmental coercion was involved in presenting them. Still others, picturing a higher, harder wall between church and state, felt the First Amendment barred both. Hanging over this collection of opinions was the Court's *Lemon* test—first announced in the 1971 decision *Lemon v. Kurtzman*—purportedly governing Establishment cases: For government action to pass constitutional muster, it must (1) have a secular *purpose*, (2) have a primary *effect* that neither advances nor inhibits religion, *and* (3) not foster excessive *entanglement* with religion.[3] In 2019, the Justices fractured over their acceptance or rejection of the *Lemon* test, reflecting a broader debate in the scholarly community over the test's merits.

American Legion v. American Humanist Association thrust the Court into a kerfuffle over the Bladensburg Peace Cross, a large World War I monument located at a busy Maryland intersection. The Cross has stood since 1925, and Maryland has owned it and the surrounding land since at least 1961. Seven Justices ultimately found that the Cross did not violate the Establishment Clause, with Justices Ginsburg and Sotomayor in dissent. But if the opinion lineup is not as frenetic as in *County of Allegheny*, the case exposed long-running disagreements on the Court about the constitutional standard for government interaction with religion, even as the Court's membership has changed with time.

The Decision

First, the facts: The Bladensburg Cross was dedicated to honor soldiers who died in World War I. Its shape was chosen in light of the rows and rows of stark wooden crosses that marked soldiers' graves during the war. This symbol, a "simple white cross," became indelibly linked to the war, featured in poetry and photographs as a central image of the conflict. Started in 1918 by a citizens' committee in Prince George's County, Maryland, the monument was completed by the American

---

[3]403 U.S. 602 (1971)

Legion in 1925. The finished monument stands thirty-two feet tall, includes the American Legion's emblem, and displays a bronze plaque "list[ing] the names of 49 local men, both Black and White, who died in the war."[4] The American Humanist Association (an atheist advocacy group whose motto is "good without a god") brought suit requesting the monument be taken down or removed to private land. The federal district court sided with the American Legion, but the US Court of Appeals for the Fourth Circuit ruled 2-1 in favor of the American Humanists.

Justice Alito wrote the majority opinion, which was joined by Chief Justice Roberts, Justice Breyer, and Justice Kavanaugh, and by Justice Kagan in part. Justices Gorsuch and Thomas concurred in the judgment, but with very different reasoning. The two dissenters were Justices Ginsburg and Sotomayor. The majority acknowledges that the cross "has long been a preeminent Christian symbol."[5] The cross's religious symbolism, however, tells only part of the story, as even symbols that retain their religious meanings may be permissible under the Establishment Clause. The majority catalogues the many crosses in popular use that enjoy secular understandings, even where a cross was originally chosen for religious reasons. The specific, secular meanings associated with the Bladensburg Cross are especially important, as this monument's shape stems from its close connection to World War I grave markers. This is key for the majority—it propels the opinion's logic at almost every turn—and it also illustrates the prominent roles context and history play in the Court's monument-centered Establishment cases.

The import of the cross's symbolic meaning—a witness to World War I heroism and sacrifice—becomes clear once the Court enunciates its legal principles, and it is here that the Court begins to show its colors and divide. As always, the case turns on the meaning of the "vexing" Establishment Clause. In the plurality sections of his opinions (i.e., those that Justice Kagan does not join and, therefore, represent

---

[4]*American Legion* decision, page 7.
[5]Ibid., page 2.

agreement among only four Justices), Justice Alito castigates the *Lemon* test as a misguided attempt to distill precedent into an orderly and predictable analytical framework. Consequently, *Lemon* has fallen out of vogue, and in some doctrinal areas the Court simply ignores it. *Lemon*'s obsolescence, says the plurality, stems not only from its doctrinal shortcomings, but from the wide range of cases the Establishment Clause covers. *Lemon* sought a unified "theory of everything" in an area ill-suited for such certainty.

Justice Alito points to four problems with *Lemon* that are particularly acute when dealing with long-standing monuments like the Bladensburg Cross (and, here, Justice Kagan joins back in): (1) identifying the original purpose of a long-standing monument is difficult; (2) monuments, with the passage of time, may take on new, changed, or varied purposes; (3) a monument's message, like its purpose, may change over time; and (4) as time imbues monuments with communal familiarity, removing them may smack of hostility toward religion. These four concerns "show that retaining established, religiously expressive monuments, symbols, and practices is quite different from erecting or adopting new ones," such that "[t]he passage of time gives rise to a strong presumption of constitutionality."[6] Thus, where monuments with a long-standing history follow in a tradition of "respect and tolerance for differing views, an honest endeavor to achieve inclusivity and nondiscrimination, and a recognition of the important role that religion plays in the lives of many Americans," they are (likely) constitutional.[7]

Concurrences from Different Perspectives

At bottom, *American Legion*'s majority opinion is relatively narrow: It upholds *this* monument, with its own, individual heritage, in *this* context. While Justice Alito casts doubt on *Lemon*'s utility for analyzing long-standing monuments, he is unable to marshal five votes

---

[6]Ibid., page 21.
[7]Ibid., page 28.

to unequivocally overturn it. However, given Justices Thomas and Gorsuch's overt skepticism about *Lemon*, it seems clear that *Lemon* will not govern cases such as this one going forward.[8] Uncertainty over that future plays out in the concurrences and dissent. For example, Justices Breyer (whose concurrence is joined by Kagan) and Kagan (who authors a solo concurrence) occupy a "moderate middle" in Religion Clauses cases when compared with Justices Ginsburg and Sotomayor.[9] These two Justices avoid rigid doctrinarism in Establishment cases, favoring instead a pragmatic, case-specific approach—and *American Legion* is no different. Citing his established belief that "there is no single formula for resolving Establishment Clause challenges," Breyer "consider[s] each case in light of the basic purpose that the Religion Clauses were meant to serve: assuring religious liberty and tolerance for all, avoiding religiously based social conflict, and maintaining that separation of church and state that allows each to flourish in its separate sphere."[10] In that vein, Breyer's concurrence pointedly notes that *American Legion* does not resolve cases involving recently erected monuments or a record of deliberate disrespect toward religious minorities by monument creators.

Justice Kagan's brief partial concurrence sounds a similar tone and is even more optimistic about *Lemon*'s longevity. Though Kagan agrees that "rigid application of the *Lemon* test does not solve every Establishment Clause problem," she "think[s] the test's focus on purposes and effects is crucial in evaluating governmental action in this sphere—as this very suit shows."[11] Like Justice Breyer, Justice Kagan praises the majority opinion's "sensitivity to and respect for this Nation's

---

[8]For further discussion, see Ronald Kahn, "Chapter Four: Constituting the Separation of Church and State," in *The Supreme Court & Constitutional Theory, 1953–1993* (Lawrence, KS: University Press of Kansas, 1994), pages 107–138; and Ronald Kahn, "God Save Us from the Coercion Test: Constitutive Decision-Making, Polity Principles, and Religious Freedom," 43 *Case-Western Reserve Law Review* 983–1020 (Spring 1993).

[9]For example, Justices Breyer and Kagan voted with the five "conservative" Justices in *Trinity Lutheran Church of Columbia, Inc. v. Comer* in 2017 and *Masterpiece Cakeshop v. Colorado Civil Rights Commission* in 2018, both Free Exercise Clause cases. (See Chapter 6 in *SCOTUS 2018*, "*Masterpiece Cakeshop* on Gay Rights Versus Religious Liberty," by Stephen Engel.)

[10]*American Legion* Breyer concurrence, page 1.

[11]*American Legion* Kagan concurrence, page 1.

pluralism, and the values of neutrality and inclusion that the First Amendment demands."[12] In her eyes, the salient question is whether a long-standing monument reflects respect and tolerance for diverse views, a genuine effort to achieve inclusivity, and recognition that religion plays a central role in many Americans' lives.

The Court's newest member, Justice Kavanaugh, pens a substantial concurrence, aiming to clarify the majority opinion and provide guidance to lower courts. He sees a "history and tradition test" at work in Justice Alito's opinion—a characterization with which Justice Breyer takes issue. Indeed, Kavanaugh argues that *Lemon* no longer applies to Establishment Clause cases at all. In its place, he offers his own analytical framework for adjudicating Establishment cases of all stripes: "If the challenged governmental practice is not coercive *and* if it (i) is rooted in history and tradition; or (ii) treats religious people, organizations, speech, or activity equally to comparable secular people, organizations, speech, or activity; or (iii) represents a permissible legislative accommodation or exemption from a generally applicable law, then there ordinarily is no Establishment Clause violation."[13]

While Justice Kavanaugh's concurrence suggests a new path for Establishment Clause cases, it appears modest when juxtaposed against the opinions of Justices Thomas and Gorsuch, who concur in the judgment only. Justice Thomas rejects the Establishment Clause's incorporation (via the Fourteenth Amendment) against the states, which dates to the 1940s—not a new idea for him, but jarring nevertheless. Based on its original meaning, as divined by Thomas, the Clause bars only the national government, not states, from endorsing or establishing religion, allowing (even anticipating) that state government will establish or endorse religion. Thus, its incorporation against the states is illogical. Thomas also suggests the Clause applies only to "laws," such that a monument would not fall within its ambit. Thomas' test for Establishment Clause violations reflects the Clause's limited scope: A plaintiff "must demonstrate that he was actually coerced by

---

[12]Ibid., page 2.
[13]*American Legion* Kavanaugh concurrence, page 4.

government conduct that shares the characteristics of an establishment as understood at the founding."[14] Actual coercion is a high bar, and were Thomas' test to go into effect, the government's power to explicitly inject religion into the public square would grow considerably greater.

Justice Gorsuch's concurrence (joined by Justice Thomas) is no less iconoclastic. Perhaps its standout facet is its transformation of coercion—the touchstone of Establishment Clause jurisprudence for prior Justices like Kennedy and Scalia—into a jurisdictional prerequisite. According to Gorsuch, plaintiffs whose only injury is offense at seeing religious monuments lack standing, a limitation on federal courts' ability to hear Establishment Clause cases. Offended observer standing, says Gorsuch, is fruit of the poisonous *Lemon* tree. He hopes that, by shelving *Lemon*, the Court can also shelve this standing theory. Thus, *American Legion* would never have reached the Court on the merits—it likely never would have reached the Court at all—instead being disposed of at an earlier, motion-to-dismiss stage. The implications of Gorsuch's concurrence are clear from his list of prototypical Establishment Clause plaintiffs—a "public school student compelled to recite a prayer," "persons denied public office because of their religious affiliations or lack of them," and individuals "denied governmental benefits because they do not practice a favored religion or any at all."[15] These plaintiffs all have in common some concrete injury stemming from coercive state action. In this regard, Justices Thomas and Gorsuch focus, even more than Justice Kavanaugh, on coercion as central to the Establishment Clause.

The Dissenters

Finally, Justices Ginsburg and Sotomayor dissent, concluding that the Bladensburg Cross's presence on public land "elevates Christianity over other faiths," and places the government's imprimatur on religion over

---

[14]*American Legion* Thomas concurrence, page 3.
[15]*American Legion* Gorsuch concurrence, pages 9–10.

irreligion.[16] Relying on governmental endorsement, not coercion, as the Establishment Clause's baseline—an approach formulated by Justice Sandra Day O'Connor in the 1980s—these Justices cannot see how an "exclusively Christian symbol… loom[ing] over public thorough-fares" would not "suggest official recognition of [Christianity's] para-mountcy."[17] Notably absent from the dissent, though, is a defense of *Lemon*, which leaves a reader wondering how much support for *Lemon* remains on the current Court.

Future Implications

American Legion's implications are hazy. The majority opinion is funda-mentally limited in scope—and while it diminishes (if not eliminates) *Lemon*'s role in long-standing monuments cases, whether this dimin-ishment spills into other Establishment cases is unsettled. The Court's continued emphasis on context seems to indicate that most Justices will proceed cautiously and incrementally, assessing each case before the Court without issuing sweeping formulae. Indeed, Justice Alito's opin-ion cites Justice Breyer's concurrence in *Van Orden v. Perry*, where the Court found constitutional a Ten Commandments monument on Texas state capitol grounds.[18] In providing the fifth vote in *Van Orden*, Justice Breyer emphasized the Religion Clauses' basic purposes—promoting tolerance, avoiding divisiveness and conflict, and recognizing both the separation and coexistence of church and state. And in rejecting a one-size-fits-all approach to these cases, Breyer saw one factor as determina-tive in long-standing monument cases: a decades-long absence of any substantial opposition to a monument (provided there is no evidence of intimidation stifling dissent). A lengthy pattern of social harmony has become a narrowly focused standard around which the Court can coalesce, resolving most cases of historical religious monuments while

---

[16]*American Legion* Ginsburg dissent, page 3.
[17]Ibid., pages 7–8.
[18]545 U.S. 667 (2005)

avoiding the critical question framing so many Establishment issues over the past decades—whither *Lemon*?

A restrained, realistic approach to Establishment cases would also comport with past opinions, in particular those of Justice O'Connor, who noted that the propriety of governmental action under the Establishment Clause depends on the "judicial interpretation of social facts."[19] "Social construction," or the Court's bidirectional considera- tion of the legal principles and social, political, and economic circum- stances of citizens' lived lives, is not unique to one area of the law, but it has heightened importance in Establishment cases.[20] In part, this also stems from another of O'Connor's contributions—the endorse- ment test, which assesses whether governmental action conveys to the reasonable observer that "adherence to a religion [is] relevant ... to a person's standing in the political community."[21] If Justice O'Connor's endorsement test does not control the Court today, it still echoes in the *American Legion* opinions—strongly in Justices Breyer and Kagan's con- currence, softly, though audibly in the majority opinion, even faintly in Justice Kavanaugh's concurrence. The endorsement test's enduring impact, though, was setting the Court's focus on the practical implica- tions of governmental action, homing in on the specific facts of specific cases and asking how and what monuments or symbols or laws com- municate to real people in the real world. Thus, as the Court contin- ues to retreat from the maximalist *Lemon* test, it becomes increasingly

---

[19]*Lynch v. Donnelly*, 465 U.S. 668 (1984) at 693–94.

[20]See Ronald Kahn, "Supreme Court Decision-Making and the Social Construction Process: Continuity in a Polarized Age," 4 *Constitutional Studies* 155–187 (2019); Ronald Kahn and Gerard Michael D'Emilio, "The Jurisprudence of Justice Scalia: Common-Law Judging Behind an Originalist Façade," in *The Conservative Revolution of Antonin Scalia*, eds. David A. Schultz and Howard Schweber (Lanham, MD: Lexington Books, 2018), pages 219–244; and Ronald Kahn, "Social Constructions, Supreme Court Reversals, and American Political Development: *Lochner, Plessy, Bowers*, but Not *Roe*," in *The Supreme Court and American Political Development*, eds. Ronald Kahn and Ken I. Kersch (Lawrence, KS: University Press of Kansas, 2006), pages 67–113.

[21]*Lynch*, 465 U.S. at 687–88.

minimalist in the Establishment Clause context—abandoning a "theory of everything" for a case-by-case approach.[22]

Notwithstanding *American Legion*'s potential narrowness, the Court has been creeping toward an Establishment Clause jurisprudence more permissive of government-endorsed displays of religiosity. The notion that coercion is a necessary part of a successful Establishment claim crops up in Justices Kavanaugh, Gorsuch, and Thomas' opinions. Alongside this is a latent tolerance principle that percolates beneath the majority opinion's surface—an attitude (likely held by at least five Justices) that if it's not too bad, if it doesn't seem like a big deal, it passes constitutional muster. So, while Justice Breyer's *Van Orden* concurrence has been highly influential of late, the Court may slowly water down this already humble opinion until "coercion," either direct or indirect, represents the Establishment Clause's threshold. The majority also notes the potential societal discord that may be wrought by removing monuments—an observation not necessarily limited to the long-standing monuments context. *American Legion*'s narrowness, then, may obfuscate a coming Establishment Clause revolution, wherein the Court places greater and greater emphasis on history, tradition, and the status quo in a growing set of Establishment cases, until we are left with little more than "coercion or bust." But such predictions are tricky business—as Court decision-making tends not to be so radical—and with the Court consistently fractured in this area there is reason to think it will remain so in the future.

So, after *American Legion*, has *Lemon* been squeezed dry? To stretch the metaphor, while its juice may be tapering to a trickle, its rind remains. From *American Legion*, it seems clear that four Justices still see some value in *Lemon*—Justice Ginsburg and Sotomayor, implicitly; Justice Kagan, as a rule of thumb; and Justice Breyer, as a jumping-off point, if not a specific test. And as long as the Court lacks five clear voices calling for *Lemon* to be stricken with the judicial red pen, the test will likely have some continuing impact, if only as a set of orienting

---

[22]Justice Alito's footnote on a taxonomy of Establishment Clause cases seems to imply that the Court should take an eclectic, rather than homogenous, approach to these issues. See *American Legion* decision, page 15 note 16.

signposts. But this much is clear: No matter the fate of *Lemon* or the religious monuments dotting the nation, the Court's approach to Establishment Clause cases remains one of cabined consensus and broad disunity, and if this persists, then the majority of Justices may continue to latch on to narrow points of agreement, proceeding case by case while arguing over the constitutional deep structure. While Maryland's old rugged cross still stands, the next new one may not.

3

Department of Commerce v. New York on the Census Citizenship Question

Brett Curry

Most Supreme Court cases are easy to pigeonhole. The legal issues they involve may be knotty and the choices before the Justices difficult, but the cases typically lend themselves to a fairly obvious taxonomy—they raise constitutional questions or call for statutory interpretation; they involve the states, Congress, or executive action; and they surround structures of government or substantive rights of individuals. But the *Department of Commerce* case combined statutory questions with constitutional ones. It required the Court to tackle issues at the intersection of legislative, executive, and judicial authority. And, while the case's constitutional dimension centered on Article I's requirement that an "actual Enumeration" of the US population be taken every ten years, notions of equal treatment under law were lurking in the background.

The census case was anomalous for another reason. When the Supreme Court agrees to hear a case, it does so only after the trial court or agency decision in question has undergone initial appellate review.

B. Curry (✉)
Georgia Southern University, Statesboro, Georgia
e-mail: bcurry@georgiasouthern.edu

© The Author(s) 2020
D. Klein and M. Marietta (eds.), *SCOTUS 2019*,
https://doi.org/10.1007/978-3-030-29956-9_3

For cases like *Department of Commerce*, that would ordinarily mean a US Court of Appeals would assess the district court decision before the Justices considered the matter. But, in the census case, the Court granted a "writ of certiorari before judgment" for the first time under Chief Justice John Roberts and leapfrogged that traditional practice.[1] It did so because of acute time pressures related to the census, making the case "of such imperative public importance as to justify deviation from normal appellate practice and to require immediate determination" by the Court.[2]

The case itself focused on a nine-word question that Secretary of Commerce Wilbur Ross instructed the Census Bureau to include on the 2020 form: "Is this person a citizen of the United States?" A number of states, localities, and advocacy groups immediately challenged this action in federal court. One basis for the challenge was that Ross' order violated the Administrative Procedure Act (APA), a federal law governing decision making by administrative agencies. Another was rooted in the Census Act, which gives the Secretary substantial discretion over the census but also requires that Congress receive ample notice of the questions to be included. Finally, opponents argued that, because its inclusion was likely to depress responses among immigrant communities, the question would prevent the census from being the "actual Enumeration" required under Article I, rendering it unconstitutional.

The government responded that the challengers lacked an appropriate basis to sue because any harm stemming from the question was speculative. And if harm existed, it would be because third parties ignored their legal responsibility to complete the form. Beyond that, the government argued the Secretary has wide discretion to oversee the census. While some might disagree with his decision to include a citizenship question, that choice deserved respect from the courts because it was not "arbitrary and capricious."

---

[1]Kevin Russell, "Overview of Supreme Court's Cert. Before Judgment Practice," SCOTUSblog, 9 February 2009.

[2]Supreme Court Rule 11.

Background of the Case

Since 1790, the United States has conducted a census each decade to allocate membership in the House of Representatives, a process required by the Constitution. More recently, census figures have assumed a critical role in parceling out federal tax dollars—for example, in fiscal year 2016 census data influenced the distribution of more than $900 billion.[3] With one estimate suggesting that asking a citizenship question might prompt 6.5 million fewer people to participate than would otherwise be the case, the stakes were undeniably significant. Though the question did not inquire about one's legal status and by law could not be used to initiate deportation, experts believed its inclusion would chill participation by noncitizen households.[4]

Yet there was ample precedent for asking about citizenship on the US census. The first such question appeared in 1820 and, with one exception, continued to be asked through 1950.[5] Starting in 1970, the Census Bureau adopted two forms—a short form that did not ask the question and a less common long questionnaire with more than 50 items, including one about citizenship.[6] After 2000, the Bureau replaced the long form with the American Community Survey (ACS), an annual assessment of roughly 3.5 million households, which includes a citizenship question. According to Secretary Ross, he added the question to the short form for 2020 because the Justice Department (DOJ) indicated census-gathered citizenship data would facilitate enforcement of the 1965 Voting Rights Act (VRA), which is intended to promote representation of minority voters. Courts hearing claims under the Act routinely require statistics on *citizen* voting-age population, as opposed to the overall population. Without a question on the census itself,

---

[3]Amy Howe, "Argument Analysis: Divided Court Seems Ready to Uphold Citizenship Question on 2020 Census," SCOTUSblog, 23 April 2019.

[4]Pete Williams, "Supreme Court to Decide if Administration Can Ask About Citizenship in 2020 Census," *NBC News*, 22 April 2019.

[5]Mithun Mansinghani, "Facts, Not Fears, Should Control Outcome of Census Citizenship Question Case," SCOTUSblog, 2 April 2019.

[6]Hans von Spakovsky, "Only in America," SCOTUSblog, 4 April 2019.

statisticians must extrapolate from ACS data that are obtained from just one in 38 households and are not always compatible with other important data.[7] According to the government, this made ACS data "subject to interpretation and manipulation that mires states in litigation over whether minority opportunity districts were appropriately drawn."[8] But skeptics viewed the DOJ letter as a pretext—as Justice Elena Kagan phrased it, "the Secretary was shopping for a need" that could justify asking the question.[9]

Though other courts were considering related litigation, US District Judge Jesse Furman presided over the main challenge to Ross' actions from his courtroom in lower Manhattan. He issued his ruling in mid-January. Scolding the Secretary for "acting irrationally," and "fail[ing] to justify significant departures from past policies and practices," Furman termed Ross' actions a "veritable smorgasbord of classic, clear cut violations" of federal law.[10]

The government asked the Court to review Furman's decision immediately. At their private conference on February 15th—the first attended by Justice Ginsburg since her cancer surgery the previous month—the Justices granted certiorari (bypassing the Court of Appeals below them) and set argument during the Court's April sitting. Specifically, they agreed to decide whether Secretary Ross' decision violated statutes related to agency decision making.[11] Soon thereafter, however, a federal judge in California issued another important ruling on the census question. Judge Richard Seeborg also concluded that Ross' actions violated federal statutes, but his decision went further. Seeborg said the citizenship question violated the Constitution's enumeration clause, since it would thwart the census' central purpose—to produce an accurate

---

[7]*Department of Commerce v. New York* oral argument transcript, page 33.

[8]Mansinghani, "Facts, Not Fears".

[9]*Department of Commerce v. New York* oral argument transcript, page 42.

[10]*State of New York*, et al. *v. United States Department of Commerce*, et al. (2019) slip opinion, page 8.

[11]Amy Howe, "Court Will Review Census Citizenship Dispute This Term," SCOTUSblog, 15 February 2019.

population count. As a result, the Court instructed the parties to expand their arguments to encompass this constitutional dimension.[12]

At the Supreme Court

At the conclusion of the Court's 82-minute oral arguments on April 23rd, the Justices were clearly divided along ideological lines. Justices Ginsburg, Breyer, Sotomayor, and Kagan expressed skepticism about Ross' reasons for adding the question. Sotomayor called it "a solution in search of a problem," while Kagan felt that "you can't read this record without sensing that this need is a contrived one."[13] The four Democratically appointed and more liberal Justices focused on the fact that Census Bureau statisticians had told Ross the question's inclusion would yield fewer responses and, potentially, less accurate information about citizenship. The conservative Republican-appointees, led by Justice Alito, questioned whether Ross' decision was unreasonable at all, much less "arbitrary and capricious," the standard for a violation of the APA required by federal law. As Alito observed, Census Bureau experts had indicated that asking the question would generate data that were 98% accurate; however, they had not identified an error rate associated with a gauge of citizenship generated by modeling non-census data. Given the Secretary's choice between "trust us…it's going to be more accurate than 98 percent" and the firmer 98%, how could it be unreasonable for him to prefer the known quantity?[14] Justice Kavanaugh noted that citizenship questions are common aspects of the census in other nations, and indeed, the United Nations recommends them. Chief Justice Roberts and Justice Gorsuch raised sympathetic questions about VRA enforcement; Gorsuch observed that some states currently

---

[12]Amy Howe, "Justices Add Constitutional Question to Citizenship Case," SCOTUSblog, 15 March 2019.

[13]Josh Gerstein and Ted Hesson, "Supreme Court Divided on Citizenship Question for Census," *Politico*, 23 April 2019.

[14]*Department of Commerce v. New York* oral argument transcript, page 48.

objecting to the question had suggested that imputing citizenship from non-census data was problematic in other pending litigation.

The five conservative Justices seemed likely to permit the question. But, several weeks after oral argument, the estranged daughter of a deceased Republican strategist complicated the picture with a number of computer hard drives. Described as the "Michelangelo of gerrymandering," Thomas Hofeller had authored a 2015 study indicating that incorporating a citizenship question on the census could ultimately "be advantageous to Republicans and non-Hispanic whites." Material in his digital files strongly resembled aspects of letters the DOJ sent to the Census Bureau articulating the need for better citizenship data to enforce the VRA.[15] Though it emerged late in the game and was swiftly rebutted by the government, this revelation seemed to undercut important parts of the administration's explanation.

The Decision and Its Impact

Chief Justice Roberts announced the Court's decision on June 27th. Like the case's underlying issues, that decision proved difficult to categorize. Parts were unanimous, while others saw different configurations of Justices rotating to comprise a majority. Ultimately, Roberts and the conservatives formed a majority to reject the idea that adding a citizenship question violated the Constitution's enumeration clause. They also found that Secretary Ross' decision was not "arbitrary and capricious" under the APA and did not offend the Census Act. These were wins for the Trump administration. But then the Chief Justice parted with his conservative allies, joining the four liberals to find that the stated justification for the question—enforcement of the VRA—was a pretext. Saying there was nothing wrong with agency heads working "to substantiate the legal basis for a preferred policy" and that "no particular step in the process stands out as inappropriate or defective,"

---

[15]Michael Wines, "Deceased G.O.P. Strategist's Hard Drives Reveal New Details on the Citizenship Question," *The New York Times*, 30 May 2019.

Roberts nonetheless found there to be a "significant mismatch between the decision the Secretary made and the rationale he provided" and said the Court could not "ignore the disconnect."[16] Many interpreted Roberts' action as strategic, a redux of his decisive 2012 vote upholding the Affordable Care Act; the decision's announcement came minutes after the Court's five conservatives declared partisan gerrymanders nonjusticiable in a highly anticipated and controversial ruling. The two decisions "gave each side plenty to fume about," leading one writer to conclude "everybody hates John Roberts."[17]

The conservatives accused the Court of overreach. Writing for himself along with Justices Gorsuch and Kavanaugh, Justice Clarence Thomas assumed Ross' decision was reviewable under the APA but objected to divining the sincerity of an otherwise adequate rationale. The Court, he said, had never before invalidated otherwise appropriate agency action on the basis of pretext. Furthermore, Roberts' holding ran counter to the traditional presumption courts make that the executive branch's actions have been legitimately performed. Thomas warned the Court's standard could have implications in other instances. Justice Alito said the challenged activity was committed to the agency's discretion by law and could not be second-guessed by courts under the APA at all.

Still, the Chief did not go as far as the liberal Justices wanted. They argued Ross' decision was arbitrary and capricious, violating the APA—to them, its pretextual nature was secondary. Roberts did not say that. His opinion even suggested that political justifications might furnish an acceptable basis for Ross' decision. He returned the matter to the agency, leading some to suggest the government could rehabilitate its justifications and ultimately win the question's inclusion. A central obstacle to that possibility seemed a practical one—whether the printing of census materials needed to commence in July or could wait until October.

The administration initially indicated it would accept defeat, but seemingly reversed itself after President Trump tweeted that the effort

[16]*Department of Commerce v. Ross* decision, pages 26–27.
[17]Gilad Edelman, "Everybody Hates John Roberts," *Washington Monthly*, 29 June 2019.

would move forward. After a few days of uncertainty, Trump spoke from the Rose Garden on July 11th to declare the administration was abandoning its quest to include the question. Flanked by Secretary Ross and Attorney General William Barr, Trump instead announced an executive order directing federal agencies to provide the Commerce Department with any pertinent administrative data that might facilitate its compilation of citizenship data outside the census—a strategy many described as a mere tweak of existing procedures.

Trump's announcement may have sealed the question's fate on the 2020 census, but the case's consequences remain immense. Opponents feared the question would lower response rates by groups such as Latinos and immigrants in areas that tend to vote Democratic. And that this, in turn, would cause states with large immigrant populations to see their share of congressional representation and federal money decrease.[18] Some have suggested the Court's ruling could be a pyrrhic victory of sorts for the challengers, given that the litigation itself may have spawned the same fear and skepticism among immigrant communities.[19]

Others have predicted litigation designed to prevent agencies from providing citizenship data to the Commerce Department[20] but, assuming the administration can obtain citizenship information in this alternative fashion, that data may well spawn changes—and legal challenges—to legislative redistricting. In a 2016 case, the Supreme Court avoided deciding whether states could fulfill the Constitution's "one person, one vote" requirement by equalizing districts by citizen population rather than total population.[21] President Trump alluded to that issue in the Rose Garden: "This information is also relevant to administering our elections. Some states may want to draw state and local

---

[18]Adam Liptak, "Supreme Court to Hear Case on Census Citizenship Question," The *New York Times*, 15 February 2019.

[19]Jessica Levinson, "Trump's Citizenship Census Question Battle is Legally Dubious. But He May Have Already Won the War," *NBC News*, 10 July 2019.

[20]@JoshMBlackman (Josh M. Blackman). *Twitter*, 7:37 p.m., 11 July 2019.

[21]*Evenwel v. Abbott* (2016) 578 U.S. ____; Justin Levitt, "Citizenship and the Census" 119 *Columbia Law Review* 1355 (2019).

legislative districts based on the voter eligible population." Attorney General Barr reiterated the point: "There is a current dispute over whether illegal aliens can be included for apportionment purposes. Depending on the resolution of that dispute, this data may be relevant to those considerations."[22] Ironically, had the government advanced these arguments in litigation, it might well have prevailed.

Department of Commerce is likely to resonate for reasons that go beyond these purposes. The case reflects debate over the proper scope of executive authority during the Trump administration. In that sense, the decision harkens back to last term's "travel ban case" in which the Court grappled with separating "the president" from "this president."[23] Viewed alongside aspects of the Court's decisions this term in *Gundy v. United States* and *Kisor v. Wilkie* (see Chapters 6 and 8), some have interpreted *Department of Commerce* to reflect the Court's growing skepticism of deference to the administrative state—skepticism that is a conservative priority. As two scholars put it, "In their quest to hand the Trump administration a political defeat on the census, the four liberal Justices unwittingly agreed to lay the groundwork for a new world in which agencies' explanations receive strict judicial oversight."[24]

Finally, the census case has also made the controversial practice of so-called nationwide injunctions more visible. Individual judges have used them to invalidate the travel restrictions litigated in *Trump v. Hawaii*, President Obama's attempt to defer removal of certain undocumented immigrants, and some three dozen other times since 2017. Critics—Attorney General Barr and Justice Thomas among them—argue such injunctions incentivize forum-shopping, disrupt the political process, can sow confusion, and are legally questionable.[25]

---

[22]"Remarks by President Trump on Citizenship and the Census," 11 July 2019.

[23]Robert Barnes, "In Travel Ban Case, Supreme Court Considers 'The President' vs. 'This President'," *The Washington Post*, 22 April 2019. See Chapter 7 of *SCOTUS 2018*, "*Trump v. Hawaii* on the Travel Ban by Anthony A. Peacock".

[24]John Yoo and James Phillips, "Roberts Thwarted Trump, but the Census Ruling Has a Second Purpose," *The Atlantic*, 11 July 2019.

[25]Nicolas Bagley and Samuel Bray, "Judges Shouldn't Have the Power to Halt Laws Nationwide," *The Atlantic*, 31 October 2018; William P. Barr, "Attorney General William P. Barr Delivers Remarks to the American Law Institute on Nationwide Injunctions," (2019); *Trump v. Hawaii* (2018) Thomas concurrence.

These blanket injunctions have a bipartisan history, with liberal groups targeting judges in Democratic states during the Trump administration and conservative causes seeking out judges in redder jurisdictions during Obama's presidency. The Court's recent decision to review the Trump administration's effort to rescind Obama-era protections for undocumented "dreamers"—an attempted rescission that (like the original Obama administration policy) has been frozen by a nationwide injunction—all but ensures continued debate over the practice in the Court's next term.[26]

---

[26]Zoe Tillman, "The Supreme Court Will Review Trump's Decision to End DACA," Buzzfeed, 28 June 2019.

4

Flowers v. Mississippi on Race in Jury Selection

Jennifer Bowie

Curtis Flowers, a black man, has been tried six times by the same prosecutor for killing four people in Mississippi in 1996. He has been on death row for the last twenty-one years. On November 2, 2018, the Supreme Court agreed to review his case, not for constitutional concerns about the death penalty or the Eighth Amendment, but instead to address whether the prosecutor improperly blocked prospective black jurors from serving on the jury. In all six trials combined, the state prosecutor used his peremptory challenges to strike 41 of 42 prospective black jurors.[1]

---

[1] *Flowers* decision, page 2.

J. Bowie (✉)
University of Richmond, Richmond, VA, USA
e-mail: jbowie@richmond.edu

© The Author(s) 2020
D. Klein and M. Marietta (eds.), *SCOTUS 2019*,
https://doi.org/10.1007/978-3-030-29956-9_4

39

Jury Selection

Historically, the jury right in the United States is attributed to the distrust early American colonists had of closed-door judicial proceedings and trials. Additionally, colonists were frustrated with the British practice of prosecuting American colonists in England in order to prevent colonists from serving on criminal juries.[2] Although the jury right is mentioned in the Declaration of Independence (paragraph 20) and Article III of the Constitution, several framers such as Patrick Henry and Thomas Jefferson believed there needed to be additional assurances against government abuses in the selection of juries.[3] The compromise the framers produced to protect against political abuses in criminal prosecutions and jury selection was the Sixth Amendment: "In all criminal prosecutions, the accused shall enjoy the right to a speedy and public trial, by an impartial jury of the State and district wherein the crime shall have been committed, which district shall have been previously ascertained by law."[4]

The significance of the *Flowers* case can best be understood in the context of how jury selection generally works in the United States. Attorneys and judges play an important role in the process of selecting jurors, with the institutional goal of obtaining an impartial jury. However, there is another underlying and often competing goal of the attorneys: to select jurors who are predisposed to be sympathetic to their side.

Although jury selection practices vary from state to state, they commonly include three steps. First, a random group of citizens within the jurisdiction is ordered by the trial court to report to the courthouse on a specified day (known as a jury summons). Next, some of those potential jurors are brought to a courtroom for a particular case, and through the process known as *voir dire* (Latin for "to speak the truth"),

---

[2]See Nancy Jean King, "American Criminal Jury," 62 *Law and Contemporary Problems* 41–68 (1999).
[3]Ibid., page 42.
[4]US Constitution Amendment VI.

the judge and attorneys ask the potential jurors questions. The purpose of *voir dire* is to determine whether the prospective jurors have biases that would interfere with their ability to render an impartial verdict. The judge may excuse potential jurors from serving on the jury based on the responses they give to the questions.

In the last part of the selection process, attorneys may challenge the remaining prospective jurors from serving. There are two types of challenges attorneys can make: *challenges for cause* and *peremptory challenges*. Challenges for cause are unlimited in number and require the attorney to argue (usually in open court) that the prospective juror cannot be impartial or is otherwise unfit to serve on the jury.[5] The judge must agree for the prospective juror to be dismissed. Alternatively, peremptory challenges do not require the approval of the judge and provide the attorneys the ability to dismiss a prospective juror from serving without stating a reason.[6] Peremptory challenges are limited—each side has a predetermined number they can exercise (which varies by jurisdiction). Because peremptory challenges can be used to strike a prospective juror for any unstated reason, their use can come into conflict with the Fourteenth Amendment's Equal Protection Clause which prohibits unequal treatment based on race.

Jury Selection and Race Discrimination

Jury selection in America has not been immune to racially discriminatory practices. Early on in our history, many states passed laws that only allowed white men to serve on juries. In several cases spanning more than a century, the Court has dealt with racial discrimination in the jury selection process, including the use of peremptory challenges. After the Fourteenth Amendment was ratified in 1868, Congress passed the Civil Rights Act of 1875, which made it a criminal offense to exclude

---

[5]See, Nancy Marder, "Juror Bias, Voir Dire, and the Judge-Jury Relationship," 90 *Chicago-Kent Law Review* 927–956 (2015), page 931.

[6]*Flowers* decision, page 8.

individuals from jury service based on race.[7] Not long after the passage of the Civil Rights Act of 1875 the Supreme Court held in *Strauder v. West Virginia* (1879) that laws which only allowed whites to serve on juries were unconstitutional because they violated the Fourteenth Amendment's Equal Protection Clause. In several cases between 1881 and 1964, the Court has reaffirmed that it is unconstitutional for states to discriminate on the basis of race in the selection of jurors.

Although it was clear from the Court's perspective that state prosecutors may not racially discriminate in the jury selection process, many prosecuting attorneys found other ways to circumvent the Court's rulings. One way was to use peremptory challenges to dismiss potential black jurors, resulting in all-white juries. As the Court explains, "In the aftermath of *Strauder*, the exclusion of black jurors became more covert and less overt—often accomplished through peremptory challenges in individual courtrooms rather than by blanket operation of the law."[8]

Then, in 1965, the Court decided in *Swain v. Alabama* that it was unconstitutional to intentionally use peremptory challenges to strike a prospective juror based on race. However, the Court in *Swain* set a virtually impossible standard for making claims of racial discrimination. The Court held that for a defendant to make a case of racial discrimination in the jury selection process, he would have to put forth evidence that the state "in case after case, whatever the circumstances, whatever the crime and whoever the defendant or the victim may be is responsible for the removal" of black prospective jurors so that no black jurors "ever serve on" juries.[9] Very few defendants could meet these enormous evidentiary requirements, and the *Swain* decision did little to combat the use of race-based discrimination in the jury selection process.

However, approximately twenty years later in *Batson v. Kentucky* (1986) the Court reaffirmed that the government may not discriminate on the basis of race "when exercising peremptory challenges" against

---

[7]Ibid., page 9.
[8]Ibid., page 11.
[9]*Swain v. Alabama*, 380 U.S. 202 (1965) at 223.

potential jurors.[10] More importantly, the Court removed the evidentiary hurdles set out in *Swain* and outlined the process for making what is now referred to as a *Batson* challenge.

According to *Batson*, a defendant may raise a challenge by relying on evidence from the state's use of peremptory challenges to exclude minority jurors at the defendant's trial. Once the defendant raises the *Batson* challenge, the burden of proof shifts to the government and the state must put forth race-neutral justifications for using its peremptory challenges on prospective black jurors. The trial court then needs to determine whether the prosecutor's justifications are legitimate or whether the use of peremptory challenges discriminated against prospective minority jurors.

The *Flowers* Case

On July 16, 1996 in the small town of Winona, Mississippi, four people were murdered at Tardy Furniture store. Almost a year later, Curtis Flowers was indicted and tried for the murders, which in Mississippi is considered a capital offense. Since 1997, Curtis Flowers has been tried six times for the Tardy Furniture murders. The first three trials each resulted in a conviction and death sentence but were later overturned by the Mississippi Supreme Court for various reasons including prosecutorial misconduct and a *Batson* violation against the government. Trials four and five resulted in hung juries that were unable to reach a unanimous verdict.

On June 18, 2010, the jury in the sixth trial found Flowers guilty of four counts of murder and he was again sentenced to death. After the initial *voir dire* process, 26 potential jurors had remained: 20 white and six black. Each side had six peremptory challenges, and the state used five of them on black prospective jurors. In the end, the jury consisted of eleven white jurors and one black juror. Flowers made a *Batson* challenge to the trial court but the judge ruled against Flowers because the

---

[10]*Batson v. Kentucky*, 376 U.S. 79 (1986).

prosecutor had put forth race-neutral reasons for exercising each peremptory challenge on the prospective black jurors.

Flowers appealed his case to the Mississippi Supreme Court. In a 5-4 decision, the Mississippi Supreme Court affirmed his conviction and affirmed the trial court's ruling that the prosecutor put forth race-neutral reasons for the peremptory strikes.[11]

The Opinion

In a 7-2 decision, the Court reversed and remanded Flowers' conviction because it found a clear *Batson* violation. Although the *Flowers* opinion is narrow in the sense that it did not make any new policy concerning the use of peremptory challenges, the decision does illustrate the complexity of *Batson* challenges. Furthermore, the Court unequivocally reaffirmed the general holding of *Batson* that the "Constitution forbids striking even a single prospective juror for discriminatory purpose."[12] The 7-2 decision was written by the newest Supreme Court justice, Brett Kavanaugh, and he was joined by the four liberal Justices (Breyer, Ginsburg, Kagan, and Sotomayor) and two conservative Justices, Roberts and Alito.

In the majority opinion, the Court spent substantial time addressing the importance of the *Batson* decision. The Court stated that "by taking steps to eradicate racial discrimination from the jury selection process, *Batson* sought to protect the rights of defendants and jurors, and to enhance public confidence in the fairness of the criminal justice system."[13] In reaffirming the *Batson* holding, the Court emphasized two main procedural and evidentiary concerns when it comes to addressing *Batson* violations.

First, the Court emphasized that defendants making *Batson* challenges are allowed to put forth an array of evidence to support their

---

[11]For an extensive case history, see the *Flowers* decision, pages 3–7.
[12]Ibid., page 18.
[13]Ibid., pages 15–16

claim. For example, evidence that may be used can range from statistical comparison of the use of peremptory challenges between black and white prospective jurors to a similar comparison of the number of questions asked of black and white prospective jurors in an effort to find reasons for exclusion. Secondly, the Court underscored that the trial court must decide whether the race-neutral reasons the prosecutor provides are the actual reasons rather than just masks for racial discrimination.

In addressing Flowers' *Batson* claim, the Court concentrated on four facts of the case. First, the Court analyzed the government's use of peremptory challenges in all six trials. The Court pointed out that in total, Mississippi used 41 of 42 peremptory challenges to strike prospective black jurors. In reviewing the history of Flowers' trials, the Court concluded that the government's use of these peremptory challenges was motivated by racial discrimination. The Court believed the prosecutor's goal was to remove as many potential black jurors as possible and that the "State appeared to proceed as if *Batson* had never been decided."[14]

Second, the Court evaluated the statistics on peremptory challenge in the most recent trial. The Court noted that the prosecutor used five of six peremptory challenges against black prospective jurors, in line with a similar pattern of exclusion of potential black jurors from the prior trials.

Third, focusing again on the sixth trial, the Court scrutinized the number of questions asked of prospective black jurors during the *voir dire* process. The majority found the prosecutor asked far more questions of prospective black jurors than of white prospective jurors, a practice known as disparate questioning. The statistics were striking. The prosecutor asked the five prospective black jurors 145 total questions compared to the twelve questions the prosecutor asked of the eleven seated white jurors. The problem with disparate questioning, the Court explained, is that "by asking a lot of questions of the black prospective jurors… a prosecutor can try to find some pretextual reason—any reason—that the prosecutor can later articulate to justify what is in

---

[14]Ibid., page 21.

reality a racially motivated strike."[15] In other words, when the prosecutor asks a disproportionate amount of questions to prospective black jurors, they will inevitably find a race-neutral reason to strike the potential black juror. Likewise, when the government does not pursue the same level of questioning of prospective white jurors, the prosecutor can "distort the record."[16] As a result, "disparity in questioning and investigation can produce a record that says little about white prospective jurors and is thereby resistant to characteristic-by-characteristic comparison of struck black jurors and seated white jurors."[17] While providing strong repudiation of the disparate questioning tactics used in this case, the Court also suggested that disparate questioning alone does not constitute a *Batson* violation.

Lastly, the Court examined in the sixth trial the discriminatory intent of the peremptory challenges, concluding that the State struck at least one potential black juror who "was similarly situated to white prospective jurors who are not struck by the state."[18] To reach this conclusion, the Court took the unusual step of comparing the prospective jurors that were struck and not struck by the government. The Court focused on four jurors: Carolyn Wright (a prospective black juror) and Pamela Chasteen, Harold Waller, and Bobby Lester (three prospective white jurors). The Court went through all the similarities Wright shared with the three white jurors. For example, Wright was pro-death penalty, had a family member who worked as a prison security guard (alluding to her pro-law enforcement disposition), knew several witnesses for the prosecution and defense, and was employed at the same Wal-Mart where Flowers' father worked. However, what confounded the Court was that Chasteen, Waller, and Lester also knew numerous witnesses in the case and family members of Flowers. While the prosecutor asked Wright several questions about how she knew various witnesses, he did not ask

---

[15]Ibid., page 25.
[16]Ibid.
[17]Ibid.
[18]Ibid., page 3.

the three white jurors similar follow-up questions.[19] The Court argued that "the side-by-side comparison of Wright to white prospective jurors who the state accepted for the jury cannot be considered in isolation in this case," concluding that striking Wright was motivated by racially discriminatory intent in violation of *Batson*.[20] These four case facts, taken together, proved decisive and the Court overturned Flowers' conviction.

The Dissent

Justice Thomas, joined in part by Justice Gorsuch, wrote the dissenting opinion. Thomas took the majority to task for reviewing the case in the first place, suggesting that they did so because of media pressure.[21] Next, Thomas went on to argue that the state of Mississippi did not purposefully discriminate when it exercised its peremptory challenges. Thomas asserted that "Each strike was supported by multiple race-neutral reasons articulated by the State at the *Batson* hearing and supported by the record."[22] In part IV of his dissent (the section Justice Gorsuch did not sign on to), Thomas strongly suggested that *Batson* was wrongly decided and should be overturned. Thomas argued that *Batson v. Kentucky* "requires that a duly convicted criminal go free because a juror was arguably deprived of his right to serve on the jury. That rule was suspect when it was announced, and I am even less confident of it today."[23] Thomas concluded his dissent with this sentiment about the *Flowers* case and the majority opinion, "If the Court's opinion today has a redeeming quality, it is this: The State is perfectly free to convict Curtis Flowers again."[24]

---

[19]Ibid.

[20]Ibid., pages 30–31.

[21]Justice Thomas dissent, page 5.

[22]Ibid., page 10.

[23]Ibid., page 33.

[24]Ibid., page 42.

Conclusion

Flowers v. Mississippi was decided on narrow grounds. Justice Kavanaugh said it best when he wrote, "we break no new legal ground. We simply enforce and reinforce *Batson* by applying it to the extraordinary facts of this case."[25] If the *Flowers* opinion does anything, it highlights the injustices of the criminal justice system, particularly the jury selection process. It also shows the Court's willingness to reaffirm *Batson* and its commitment to holding states accountable for using peremptory challenges in a discriminatory fashion. However, critics of the Court's opinion argue that a broader decision could have helped others who face racial discrimination in the jury selection process.[26] While it is unusual for the Court to decide a case that depends so heavily on the facts, perhaps the Court did so as a reminder that "Equal justice under law requires a criminal trial free of racial discrimination in the jury selection process."[27] At this point while we do not know what is in store next for Flowers' case what we do know is this: The same prosecutor gets to decide whether to try Curtis Flowers again.

---

[25] *Flowers* decision, page 3.

[26] See David Leonhardt, "Clarence Thomas vs. the Evidence," *The New York Times*, 3 July 2019. See also Episode 14 of the "In the Dark" podcast.

[27] *Flowers* decision, page 15.

5

Gamble v. U.S. on Double Jeopardy

Rory K. Little

In 1791, ten of the twelve constitutional amendments proposed in the First Congress were ratified as a Bill of Rights to allay concerns that the new Federal government would violate the rights of "the People." The Fifth Amendment contained this awkward, written-by-Committee sentence, now referred to as the Double Jeopardy Clause: "nor shall any person be subject for the same offense to be twice put in jeopardy of life or limb."

Over two centuries later, Terance Martez Gamble was prosecuted by Alabama under a state law making it illegal for anyone previously convicted of a crime of violence to possess a firearm. Gamble pled guilty and later received a year in prison. Federal prosecutors then indicted him "for the same instance of possession" under a federal law that also prohibits convicted felons from possessing a firearm. Gamble argued that the federal prosecution for this "same offence" violated the Double Jeopardy Clause. His motion was denied, and Gamble was sentenced federally to almost three additional prison years.

R. K. Little (✉)
U.C. Hastings College of the Law, San Francisco, CA, USA
e-mail: littler@uchastings.edu

© The Author(s) 2020
D. Klein and M. Marietta (eds.), *SCOTUS 2019*,
https://doi.org/10.1007/978-3-030-29956-9_5

On June 17, 2019, the US Supreme Court rejected Gamble's double jeopardy argument and affirmed his federal conviction. The Justices upheld a long line of precedents holding that because the federal and State governments are "separate sovereigns," they may both prosecute a person for the same criminal act. Rather than overrule those precedents, the majority decided to stick with "over 170 years" of cases holding that state and federal prosecutions for the same crime are not double jeopardy because when crimes are prosecuted by separate sovereigns, they are automatically *different* offenses.

The Majority Opinion

The only question at issue in *Gamble* was whether to follow the "separate sovereigns" precedents. Justice Samuel Alito, a former federal prosecutor confirmed to the Court in 2006 under President George W. Bush, began his majority opinion by noting that the Court's double jeopardy precedents describe a "complex" body of law.[1] But he found the separate sovereigns question to be easy, because the constitutional text does not explicitly prohibit it and the rule is supported by history, precedent, and policy. Gamble offered some contrary textual evidence from the Constitution's drafting debates, as well as cases from British and American history. But Justice Alito's opinion examined the seventeenth- and eighteenth-century British cases "in some detail" and found that they yielded conflicting inferences about the meaning of the Clause— the majority described the history as "feeble," "a muddle," "equivocal and downright harmful" to Gamble's arguments.[2] Meanwhile, "almost two centuries of [Supreme Court] precedent" had concluded that prosecutions for the same conduct by a state and the federal government,

---

[1]Professor Akhil Reed Amar has written that "Supreme Court case law is full of double jeopardy double talk." Amar, "Double Jeopardy Law Made Simple," 106 *Yale Law Journal* 1087 (1997).

[2]*Gamble* decision, pages 2, 12.

or even by two separate states, do not contravene the Double Jeopardy Clause.[3]

Justice Alito offered a theme of "duality of harms" to support the Court's line of precedents going back to 1852. In *Moore v. Illinois*, the Court had said that the murder of a federal Marshal could be prosecuted by both a state and the federal government, because the criminal act offended both a state's general interest in criminalizing violence and the *different* federal interest of protecting federal officials from attack. This same "duality of harms" idea underlies the federal enforcement of civil rights laws in the twentieth century, when some state prosecutions were viewed as ineffective, intentionally weak, or non-existent. Consider, for example, the federal prosecution of state law enforcement officers who killed a young black man in Georgia in 1943, and the federal prosecution of police officers who were caught on tape viciously beating Rodney King in Los Angeles in 1991.[4]

Today, the strong federal enforcement of criminal civil rights statutes in cases of state inaction is generally celebrated. Justice Alito's opinion addressed the idea in a less explosive context of "crimes involving Americans abroad"—if an American were murdered in another country, we might "lack confidence in the competence or honesty of the other county's legal system" and thus want a second prosecution for the same crime.[5] International law as well as our own would unhesitatingly endorse such dual prosecutions. For purposes of the *Gamble* Court, foreign governments, the federal government, and state governments are equally "sovereign" as independent prosecutors.

But even if persuasive, such policy arguments say nothing about a necessary meaning of the constitutional text. By contrast, we know with some confidence that the constitutional Framers and state ratifiers in 1791 intended the Bill of Rights to restrict only the federal government. Chief Justice Marshall, who was present at the Framing as a young Congressman, told us this himself in *Barron v. Baltimore*: the Bill

---

[3]Ibid., page 28.
[4]*Screws v. United States*, 325 U.S. 91 (1945); *Koon v. United States*, 518 U.S. 81 (1996).
[5]*Gamble* decision, page 7.

of Rights "must be understood as restraining the power of the General [federal] Government, not as applicable to the States."[6] Indeed, restraining the federal government, not limiting the States, was the very point of so quickly adding the first ten amendments to the Constitution.

But then in 1868, the Fourteenth Amendment was added to the Constitution, extending the protections of "due process" to all persons against state actions. This led to a twentieth century line of cases holding that the Bill of Rights is "incorporated" into the Fourteenth Amendment's constitutional protection, thereby extending the Bill of Rights as protection against actions of *state* governments.[7] With the Double Jeopardy Clause having been incorporated to apply against the states fifty years ago,[8] and all Justices agreeing today that state and federal governments are governed alike by the Clause, it seems anomalous to say that separate state and federal sovereigns can still prosecute for the same offense. But the *Gamble* majority dismissed this "incorporation changes everything argument" in a few paragraphs, noting that the meaning of "same offense" that allows dual-sovereign prosecutions to be counted as different has been embraced by the Court both before and after incorporation. There is "no logical reason," said the majority, why the application of due process to the states should be extended to blocking prosecutions by different sovereigns. State and federal crimes are simply viewed as constitutionally different, so that the constitutional "same offence" prohibition does not apply even for the same criminal conduct.

The *Gamble* majority explains that the "dual sovereignty" theory of federalism—that both the federal government and state governments are "sovereign" even within the same geographic territory—is "foundational" to the American constitutional system. It "often results in two layers of regulation" over the same subject matter, both by States and the federal government (e.g., taxation or perhaps more controversially, the sale of marijuana). Justice Alito (a sometimes harsh critic of those

---

[6]32 U.S. 243, 247 (1833).
[7]See the discussion of incorporation in *Timbs v. U.S.* in Chapter 12.
[8]*Benton v. Maryland* (1969).

who disagree with him) wrote that the dissenters' argument that "the People" of America constitute a unitary "Whole" sovereign that can tolerate only a single prosecution for a crime, "fundamentally misunderstands the governmental structure established by our Constitution." "The United States is a *federal* republic; it is not... a unitary state like the United Kingdom."[9]

The bulk of Justice Alito's opinion in *Gamble* is devoted to demonstrating that there is no "special justification" for overcoming "*numerous major decisions of this Court spanning 170 years.*"[10] This is of course the doctrine of *stare decisis*, which counsels against overruling precedents merely because one disagrees with them. Roughly 20 of Justice Alito's 31 pages were devoted to showing that none of Gamble's arguments were strong enough to "blunt the force of *stare decisis.*"

The Dissents

The Supreme Court's history includes many examples of rulings that were foreshadowed in prescient dissents—such as whether wiretapping should be governed by the Fourth Amendment or whether "separate but equal" violates the Fourteenth Amendment.[11] Careful students of the law cannot fully understand the meaning of majority opinions without also reading the dissents.

Justices Ginsburg and Gorsuch wrote separate dissents in *Gamble*. These two Justices are generally viewed as ideologically far apart. Yet they both focused intensely on the Bill of Rights' ethic of protecting "individual liberty" and each argued that the constitutionality of two prosecutions for the same crime should be viewed *from the perspective of the individual defendant*, not that of the government. Justice Gorsuch opined that the "ordinary reader" of the Double Jeopardy Clause would

---

[9]*Gamble* decision, page 10.

[10]Ibid., page 12 (emphases in original).

[11]See *Olmstead v. United States*, 277 U.S. 436, 471 (1928, Brandeis dissenting), overruled in *Katz v. United States*, 389 U.S. 347 (1967); *Plessy v. Ferguson*, 163 U.S. 537, 552 (1896, Harlan dissenting), overruled in *Brown v. Board of Education*, 347 U.S. 483 (1954).

be surprised to learn that he or she could be double-punished by both the state and federal governments for the same criminal conduct. "Really?" concluded this section of Gorsuch's dissent.

Justice Gorsuch also claimed that "the Framers understood" that the Double Jeopardy Clause "as originally adopted" would bar successive prosecutions by two separate sovereigns. His argument was that the Constitution divided government between two sovereigns, state and federal, not to *multiply* governmental power but to *diffuse* it, and thereby protect the individual liberty of all. But Gorsuch's dissent never discusses the accepted original understanding of the Framers that the Bill of Rights would bind only the federal government, not the States.

Justice Ginsburg's dissent does address this and argues that the twentieth-century incorporation of the Double Jeopardy Clause against the states renders the Framer's 1791 understanding "irrelevant." Meanwhile, both dissents stressed that the enormous expansion of federal criminal statutes in recent years should give the Court pause, because virtually all criminal conduct today is "dual jurisdictional" and can be charged under federal and state laws alike.[12] Thus, the dangers of abuse by "dual prosecutions" are much greater than even 50 years ago, let alone at the time of the Constitution's framing.

Justice Gorsuch also noted, accurately, that the 1852 *Moore* case (which first explicitly approved separate-sovereign prosecutions) interpreted the Constitution "in the name of protecting slavery and slave-owners." This indeed might be viewed as undermining anything said in that opinion. But the majority countered that the "separate sovereigns" rule has been followed in many other cases and contexts, and the strength of this *line* of decisions supports its endorsement today.

Both ideologically different dissenters agreed that the doctrine of *stare decisis* ought not sustain the precedents allowing dual-sovereign prosecutions. Justice Gorsuch recited four factors that the Court traditionally examines when considering to overrule a precedent and noted that *stare decisis* is "at its weakest" in constitutional (as opposed to

---

[12]See Rory K. Little, "The Federal Death Penalty," 26 *Fordham Urban Law Journal* 347, 413 (1999).

statutory) cases. Because a doctrine that allows dual prosecutions threatens individual liberty and seems to violate the constitutional text as well as policy, Justice Ginsburg and Gorsuch agreed that the Court should overrule.

The impulse to abandon *stare decisis* here is strong, in light of potential abuses. But that doctrine is hardly a clear or consistent one. Significantly, only a month earlier these same two Justices had flatly disagreed about the application of *stare decisis*—and nine days after *Gamble* they disagreed again.[13] These varying applications of *stare decisis* simply underline the unfortunate reality that the doctrine is, at best, uncertain, ill defined, and lacks any specific predictive power.

Justice Thomas: A New *Stare Decisis* Standard?

In an opinion concurring in the majority's ruling, Justice Thomas offered a different rule for *stare decisis*, argued that the Court's cautious multi-factor analysis for when to overrule a precedent is an "attempt to quantify the unquantifiable." Thomas instead asserted that the Court should simply ask whether a prior decision is "demonstrably erroneous." If so, Thomas says they should overrule it. Yet the consistently pro-prosecution Justice Thomas did not find his standard met in this case, so he agreed to affirm Gamble's conviction. But he then linked his different view of the power of precedent directly to abortion, signaling his substantive view on that explosive question well beyond any issue in *Gamble*. No other member of the *Gamble* Court mentioned abortion, and Justice Thomas' lone view was not endorsed by any other Justice. Still, the threat is apparent: *stare decisis* may not carry the day when the issue of whether to affirm or overrule *Roe v. Wade* reaches the Court.

---

[13]*Franchise Tax Board of Calif. v. Hyatt* (2019), see Chapter 13; *Kisor v. Wilkie* (2019), see Chapter 8.

Thoughts on Three Broader Issues

Separate sovereigns: The question of who exactly counts as a "sovereign" is complex in our unique constitutional system. States were historically "sovereign," like independent nations, once they declared their independence from Great Britain in 1776. A decade later, those sovereign States agreed to give up some—but not all—of their sovereignty to an overarching federal authority. Recently retired Justice Kennedy famously described this as a revolutionary idea, "splitting the atom of sovereignty" for residents of the same territory between two separate governmental structures.

At the same time, we generally understand that county and municipal governments in the United States are not "sovereign," despite also having significant authority over individuals within the same borders. Instead, they are viewed as mere "subdivisions" of their states—but states are not "subdivisions" of the federal government. At the other extreme, foreign nations are universally accepted as wholly and independently sovereign (although the European Union may give pause here). And it is well-accepted that even under the constitutional Double Jeopardy Clause, a criminal prosecution in a foreign country should have no effect on the validity of a criminal prosecution here, even if for the same conduct. Imagine, for example, a foreign terrorist bombing of a U.S. embassy—would an acquittal, or a conviction, in Iraq prevent us from constitutionally prosecuting the bombers here?

"Same offense": Similarly, whether "same offence" ought to mean something broader like "same conduct" or "the same blameworthy event" has been debated for some time.[14] The Supreme Court itself has flip-flopped over the years. In *Gamble*, all the Justices appeared to accept a relatively narrow "same exact elements" definition: if two criminal statutes each have one factual "element" that the other does not, then the crimes are not "the same offense." Both crimes may constitutionally be charged by the same sovereign even though only a single

---

[14]See George C. Thomas III, "A Blameworthy Act Approach to the Double Jeopardy Same Offense Problem," 83 *California Law Review* 1027 (1995).

criminal act is at issue. This strikes some as unfair when the two criminal statutes seem remarkably similar, differing only in some tangential detail. Consider, for example, the prosecution of one person for a single drug sale under three different statutes—selling without a license, selling something unlawful, and selling near a school—followed by the imposition of three *consecutive* prison terms, one for each "offense." This is where the modern "explosion" of criminal laws at the state and federal levels, in ever-more detail while still addressing the same misconduct, strikes some as requiring more protection from double prosecutions. But as the majority opinion noted, that concern is misdirected when aimed at the "dual sovereignty" doctrine, so long as a narrow "same offense" definition is maintained. Eliminating a "dual sovereignty" exception to Double Jeopardy would do nothing to trim the proliferation of criminal laws with slightly different elements, which then allow the application of multiple prosecutions to the same criminal conduct.

Justice Alito's opinion in *Gamble* concluded by noting that Gamble had not argued for a "revolutionary assault" on the narrow "same offense" doctrine. But it is perhaps that doctrine that leads to the unfairness and abuses that some perceive in separate-sovereign prosecutions. Some of the briefs filed in *Gamble* argued that the "same offense" assumption will be wrong in almost all state-federal contexts, because federal crimes will always require some additional "federal" element that state crimes do not. If that is true, then the identity of the "sovereign" that is prosecuting may never matter, because no two criminal statutes are ever "the same."

Stare decisis: Finally, the *Gamble* Court's discussion of *stare decisis* has broader significance, because many fear that the appointment of new conservative Justices threatens deeply sensitive Supreme Court precedents such as *Roe v. Wade*.[15] The 2018–2019 Term of the Supreme Court saw at least six cases in which the Court considered whether to overrule precedents, and the results were inconsistent: overrule in two, suggested future overruling in two others, and stick to precedent in

---

[15]*Roe v. Wade*, 410 U.S. 113 (1973).

two more. Some see this general debate as far more significant than any single substantive doctrine.

The fact that Justice Alito, who is perceived to be quite conservative, wrote the *Gamble* opinion strongly adhering to precedent, may prove significant. Or perhaps not, as Justice Alito has joined his conservative brethren in voting to overrule in other contexts. The fact is, the doctrine of *stare decisis* seems quite manipulable.[16] Indeed, in *Gamble*, Justices of opposite ideological persuasions voted together, yet on *both* sides of the debate; liberals and conservatives voted together, but in opposite directions on the question of overruling precedent. This demonstrates at best confusion, and at worst a lack of principled guidance. When Justice Kagan asked this Term whether there are any "principles about precedents at all," the answer may simply be "no." [17]

Justice Gorsuch stressed in his *Gamble* dissent that "the world has changed" since dual-sovereignty cases were decided, such that "*stare decisis* can lose its force." With extreme anti-abortion statutes expected to reach the Supreme Court in the next two years, we will see whether the massive structural and cultural changes in our world since *Roe* was decided render the force of *stare decisis* weaker, stronger, or to the dismay of many, simply irrelevant.

---

[16]Compare Alito writing to overrule a precedent in *Janus v. AFSCME* (2018) (See *SCOTUS 2018*), versus Justice Alito dissenting in *Arizona v. Gant*, 556 U.S. 332 (2009) to bemoan the majority's overruling of precedent.

[17]*Knick v. Township of Scott* (2019) Kagan dissenting, page 18.

6

Gundy v. U.S. on Delegation of Power

Gary Lawson

The civics-book model of American government says that the legislature legislates, the executive executes, and the judiciary judges. Some state constitutions make that principle explicit; for example, the Massachusetts Constitution of 1780, the country's oldest still-functioning constitution, says that "[i]n the government of this Commonwealth, the legislative department shall never exercise the executive and judicial powers, or either of them: The executive shall never exercise the legislative and judicial powers, or either of them: The judicial shall never exercise the legislative and executive powers, or either of them: to the end it may be a government of laws and not of men." The US Constitution contains no such explicit "separation of powers" clause, but it accomplishes the same result by granting only specific powers to each institution of the national government: The Congress is vested with "[a]ll legislative Powers herein granted," the President is given the "executive Power," and the federal courts are given the "judicial Power." The President, to be sure, is given an important role in the

G. Lawson (✉)
Boston University School of Law, Boston, MA, USA
e-mail: glawson@bu.edu

© The Author(s) 2020
D. Klein and M. Marietta (eds.), *SCOTUS 2019*,
https://doi.org/10.1007/978-3-030-29956-9_6

59

legislative process; congressional enactments do not become law unless the President signs them or Congress overrides a presidential veto. But the President cannot make a law unilaterally; all laws have to start with Congress. Everyone agrees about this.

But what does it mean to exercise "legislative" power? Suppose Congress passes a law telling an executive official, such as the President or the Attorney General, to "go forth and do good" or to "serve the public interest"? Is that really an exercise of "legislative" power? Would action by the President or the Attorney General pursuant to this law really be an exercise of "executive" rather than legislative power? Or are there certain decisions that just have to be made by Congress and that cannot be left to presidents and attorneys general (or courts) under vague congressional instructions to do good or to be reasonable?

This question—known doctrinally as the problem of delegation, or non-delegation, or non-subdelegation, of legislative power—was asked and left largely unanswered by the Supreme Court in *Gundy v. U.S.*, decided on June 20, 2019. The 4-1-3 decision produced no majority opinion. (Why only eight votes when there are nine Justices? Because the case was argued to the Supreme Court on October 2, 2018, and Justice Brett Kavanagh was sworn in on October 5, 2018, so he did not participate in the decision.) More importantly, the "1-3" in that voting lineup expressed a willingness on the part of at least four Justices to reconsider, in a fundamental way, the Supreme Court's approach to delegation questions in a future case. If Justice Kavanaugh is prepared to join that party down the road, *Gundy* may prove to be a harbinger of very important developments in constitutional law. In the long term, notwithstanding its inconclusive outcome, it may prove to be among the most important cases of the year.

The Delegation Question in Historical Context

The delegation question is as old as the country. In 1791, Congress vigorously debated whether it could, without unconstitutionally delegating legislative power, leave to the President the decision where to locate postal roads or whether Congress had to specify the paths of the postal carriers. (The final statute in 1792 designated, town by town, the precise path of the post roads.)[1] In the two years before that debate, Congress had, without any controversy or constitutional challenge, given the President very broad authority over military pensions and trade with Indians, including a statute instructing the President to issue licenses for trade with Indian tribes "to any proper person," with no explanation of what made a person "proper."[2]

In 1825, in its first case involving the delegation doctrine, the Supreme Court declared that "[i]t will not be contended that Congress can delegate to the Courts, or to any other tribunals, powers which are strictly and exclusively legislative." However, the Court upheld a provision allowing the federal courts to make such changes or alterations in statutorily prescribed procedural forms "as the ... Courts ... shall, in their discretion, deem expedient."[3] Over the next century, the courts considered numerous challenges to laws giving other actors broad power on matters ranging from tariffs on imports to the use of public forests to standards of purity, quality, and fitness for imported tea. All of the grants of authority in these cases were upheld against constitutional challenges, though each time the Court emphasized that the inquiry was a serious one. Indeed, in some early twentieth-century decisions that often escape notice, the Court flatly held unconstitutional a delegation to the courts to define the terms of a criminal law[4] and delegations to state legislatures to define the terms of federal admiralty law.[5]

The first cases finding unconstitutional delegations to the President or administrative agencies occurred in 1935, when the Court held unconstitutional two provisions of the National Industrial Recovery Act, one of the centerpieces of the New Deal, that gave the President the power to approve or set codes of conduct for industries, subject only to very vague (and at times contradictory) exhortations to pursue certain

---

[1]See Gary Lawson and Guy Seidman, *"A Great Power of Attorney": Understanding the Fiduciary Constitution* (Lawrence, KS: University Press of Kansas, 2017), pages 118–122.

[2]Act of July 22, 1790, ch. XXXIII, § 1, 1 Stat. 137.

[3]*Wayman v. Southard*, 23 U.S. (10 Wheat.) 1 (1825).

[4]See *United States v. L. Cohen Grocery Store Co.*, 255 U.S. 81 (1921).

[5]See *Knickerbocker Ice Co. v. Stewart*, 253 U.S. 149 (1920).

policy goals. The Court said of the most sweeping of those provisions: "It supplies no standards for any trade, industry or activity. It does not undertake to prescribe rules of conduct to be applied to particular states of fact determined by appropriate administrative procedure. Instead of prescribing rules of conduct, it authorizes the making of codes to prescribe them."[6]

Those were the last times that the Court has found delegations to executive agents unconstitutional. In 1937, in the midst of the Great Depression and following a 1936 electoral landslide for President Roosevelt and pro-New Deal legislators, the Court began backtracking from a wide range of doctrines that had limited congressional power, including the delegation doctrine. Cases over the next decade approved, without much concern, statutes such as those giving the Federal Communications Commission power to issue broadcast licenses "if public convenience, interest, or necessity will be served thereby," giving the World War II federal Price Administrator power to fix prices which "in his judgment will be generally fair and equitable," and giving the Securities and Exchange Commission power to determine whether certain corporate structures "unduly or unnecessarily complicate the structure, or unfairly or inequitably distribute voting power among security holders."[7]

Those precedents from the 1930s and 1940s have since been considered a fortiori justifications for every other statute that has been challenged on delegation grounds. (If those broader delegations were acceptable, then the many smaller ones must be as well.) As Justice Scalia put it in 1989: "What legislated standard, one must wonder, can possibly be too vague to survive judicial scrutiny, when we have repeatedly upheld, in various contexts, a 'public interest' standard?"[8] The eight-Justice majority in that 1989 case,[9] which upheld a very

---

[6]*A.L.A. Schechter Poultry Corp. v. United States*, 295 U.S. 495 (1935), at 541.

[7]See *National Broadcasting Co. v. United States*, 319 U.S. 190 (1943); *Yakus v. United States*, 321 U.S. 414 (1944); *American Power & Light Co. v. SEC*, 329 U.S. 90 (1946).

[8]*Mistretta v. United States*, 488 U.S. 361 (1989), at 416 (Scalia dissent).

[9]Justice Scalia dissented on a technical ground involving the particular agency at issue, but he agreed fully with the majority's general approach to delegation questions.

broad delegation to the US Sentencing Commission to determine the appropriate punishments for federal crimes, summarized modern law as requiring only that Congress identify an "intelligible principle" to guide the exercise of executive discretion. The decision added that in "[a]pplying this 'intelligible principle' test to congressional delegations, our jurisprudence has been driven by a practical understanding that in our increasingly complex society, replete with ever changing and more technical problems, Congress simply cannot do its job absent an ability to delegate power under broad general directives."[10] In other words, constitutional concerns about delegation need to give way to (as one of the chief architects of the New Deal put it in 1938) "the exigencies of governance."[11] In the past thirty years, the Court has steadfastly resisted a series of invitations to carve out enclaves of stricter enforcement of delegation norms for such things as criminal law, taxation, the military death penalty, or cases in which the agency given discretion had not bound its own discretion with internal rules. From 1989 to 2002, when these cases were decided, the combined vote of the Justices of the Supreme Court was 53-0 against the delegation challenges to federal laws.

The Unlikely Saga of Herman Gundy

In 2006, Congress passed a statute requiring sex offenders to register in any state in which they reside, work, or study. Failure to register, or to keep the registration current, is a federal crime subject to a ten-year prison sentence. Herman Gundy pleaded guilty to a sex offense in 2005. Seven years later, after being released from prison, he moved to New York, failed to register, and was tried and convicted for that crime. But did the 2006 law require registration for people who had been found guilty of sex offenses *before* the law took effect?

---

[10]*Mistretta*, 488 U.S. at 372.

[11]James Landis, *The Administrative Process* (New Haven, CT: Yale University Press, 1938), page 2.

The statute itself did not decide that question. Instead, it said "The Attorney General shall have the authority to specify the applicability of the requirements of this subchapter to sex offenders convicted before the enactment of this chapter…"[12] Could Congress let the Attorney General, an executive official, determine whether a federal criminal law applies to people like Gundy?

Numerous challenges to this provision were brought in the federal courts claiming an unconstitutional delegation. Every single federal court of appeals to consider that question—eleven in all, out of a total of thirteen federal courts of appeals—found the statute constitutional under the Court's existing delegation precedents. Indeed, by the time that Herman Gundy's case reached the Second Circuit Court of Appeals in New York, the issue was so firmly settled that the court brushed off Gundy's claim in a brusque footnote and did not even publish its opinion. (Courts often do not publish their opinions when they don't consider them of any general interest to the legal community.)

Gundy asked the Supreme Court to hear his case. The US government did not even bother to file a response to Gundy's petition to the Supreme Court, indicating the government's confidence that the matter was so settled and so unimportant that there was no chance that the Supreme Court would want to hear Gundy's case. To the astonishment of many observers, the Supreme Court requested a response from the government and then agreed to hear the case.

With no disagreement among the lower courts to resolve, why would the Supreme Court take Gundy's case unless it was prepared to say something very significant about the long-dormant delegation doctrine?

With that question in mind, thirteen organizations filed friend-of-the-Court briefs in the case—all of them on the side of Gundy, though a few of those briefs urged the Court to decide the case in favor of Gundy on very narrow grounds, perhaps limited only to criminal cases and/or to statutes in which the law literally says nothing, not even a vague injunction to pursue "the public interest," about the scope of the agent's discretion. The concern (or fear) of some of these organizations,

---

[12]34 U.S.C. § 20913(d) (2012).

and of the US government, was that a broad-ranging resurrection of the delegation doctrine might call into question some fundamental features of modern government. Many of the most important statutes in the modern administrative state, on matters ranging from environmental law to labor law, read much like the statutes upheld during the New Deal: They grant very broad discretion to administrative agencies or the President, subject only to vague injunctions to pursue the public interest, promote public health, and the like. A strict, or even moderately strict, enforcement of a delegation principle might require many of these statutes to be rewritten.

Gundy lost, but in a way that leaves everyone unsatisfied. Four Justices—Kagan, Ginsburg, Breyer, and Sotomayor—concluded that the statute giving authority to the Attorney General "easily passes constitutional muster."[13] That plurality of Justices agreed that if the statute really gave the Attorney General "plenary power" to require pre-Act sex offenders to register or not, then the Court would "face a nondelegation question." That does not mean that the plurality would have found such a statute unconstitutional; it means only that they would have thought the question interesting. The plurality did not think that the statute even posed an interesting question, because they concluded that the statute's context and history indicated that the Attorney General did not have completely unfettered discretion to decide who was subject to registration requirements. Instead, they read the statute implicitly to require the Attorney General to make everyone register as soon as, and through whatever means were, "feasible." If that is really what the statute said, then the Court's existing precedents would pretty clearly allow it to stand; the US Code is filled with similar injunctions to agencies to accomplish various ends "to the extent feasible." As the four Justices said after briefly surveying the many cases upholding sweeping delegations to agencies: "That statutory authority, as compared to the delegations we have upheld in the past, is distinctly small-bore."[14]

---

[13]*Gundy* plurality, page 1.
[14]Ibid., page 17.

Justice Gorsuch, writing for himself, Justice Thomas, and Chief Justice Roberts, vigorously dissented. The dissenters disagreed that one could read a "register people as fast as feasible" requirement into the statute, and without that kind of constraint, they thought the statute clearly unconstitutional. More significantly, the dissenting Justices suggested that the time may be ripe for reconsideration of the modern Court's whole approach to delegation questions. The dissenting opinion contains a lengthy discussion (the dissent is twice as long as the plurality) about first principles of government, the vital role of legislative responsibility, and the dangers to the entire constitutional structure from excessive grants of discretion to executive or judicial agents. It vigorously criticizes the post-New Deal cases for latching too literally onto the idea of finding in statutes an "intelligible principle" to guide administrative discretion as the key to delegation analysis. The dissent would instead ask whether the statute, in order to be valid, leaves only details to be filled in by executive or judicial agents, or makes laws conditional on fact-finding (with the legislature specifying which facts need to be found and by whom), or simply clarifies authority that executive or judicial agents already possess. This approach is vastly different from the consensus approach of the past 85 years.

Three Justices, however, are two less than five, and it would take five to make any major alterations in current doctrine. What about Justices Alito and Kavanaugh?

Justice Kavanaugh did not participate in the *Gundy* case because had not yet joined the Court when the oral arguments were heard in early October. Justice Alito voted to affirm Gundy's conviction, but he did not join or endorse the plurality's reaffirmation of existing law. His short (three paragraphs) but intriguing opinion explained: "If a majority of this Court were willing to reconsider the approach we have taken for the past 84 years, I would support that effort. But because a majority is not willing to do that, it would be freakish to single out the provision at issue here for special treatment."[15]

---

[15] *Gundy* Alito concurrence, page 1.

In other words, if Justice Kavanaugh had been a fourth vote to reconsider the Court's delegation jurisprudence, Justice Alito would have considered being the fifth.

Then What?

Gundy's lawyers did not ask the Supreme Court to reconsider 84 years of precedent. They framed their argument within the precedents that have guided the Court for the past century, focusing on the absence of any language in the statute appearing to limit the Attorney General's discretion. That was an eminently responsible course of action; if your client is facing ten years of jail time, you make the arguments that you think give you the best chance at five votes for some kind of ruling—any kind of ruling—in favor of your client, and there was nothing in the prior case law to suggest that there were five votes for a broad-based reconsideration of the delegation doctrine. That is no longer true. *Gundy* makes possible—indeed almost invites—future delegation-based challenges to congressional laws that are explicitly framed as efforts to reformulate the doctrine. Assuming that five Justices are (or remain) willing to go that route, the big question is: If not the "intelligible principle" inquiry, then what? Justice Gorsuch's three-part standard (allowing delegation only if conditioned on specific fact-finding, clarifying existing authority, or adding details)? And how much of the modern administrative state would that (or any other) approach to delegation call into question?

The dissenters in *Gundy* were keenly aware of this concern:

Nor would enforcing the Constitution's demands spell doom for what some call the "administrative state." The separation of powers does not prohibit any particular policy outcome, let alone dictate any conclusion about the proper size and scope of government. Instead, it is a procedural guarantee that requires Congress to assemble a social consensus before choosing our nation's course on policy questions … Congress … may always authorize executive branch officials to fill in even a large number of details, to find facts that trigger the generally applicable rule of conduct specified in a statute, or to exercise non-legislative powers. Congress can also commission agencies or other experts to study and recommend legislative language. Respecting the separation of powers forecloses no substantive outcomes. It only requires us to respect along the way one of the most vital of the procedural protections of individual liberty found in our Constitution.[16]

Time will tell if we ever have occasion to test those assumptions.

---

[16] *Gundy* Gorsuch dissent, pages 26–27.

7

U.S. v. Haymond on Re-imprisonment Without a Jury Trial

Stephen Simon

Andre Haymond was sentenced by a federal court to a five-year prison term without the benefit of a jury trial. Instead, a judge found him guilty of the charged offense after an evidentiary hearing. In *U.S. v. Haymond*, the Supreme Court held that the sentence violated Haymond's Sixth Amendment right to a jury trial. It might seem obvious that a judge may not send an individual to prison without a trial. However, it happens all the time. After individuals convicted of crimes complete a term in prison, they are commonly subject to a period of "supervised release," which conditions their continued liberty on a variety of requirements, including that they did not commit additional crimes. If the government believes that a person on supervised release has violated one or more of the requirements, it may seek a term of re-imprisonment. Defendants in this circumstance, like Haymond, are not afforded another trial in which guilt must be demonstrated "beyond a reasonable doubt" to a jury; their cases are decided by judges

S. Simon (✉)
University of Richmond, Richmond, VA, USA
e-mail: ssimon@richmond.edu

© The Author(s) 2020
D. Klein and M. Marietta (eds.), *SCOTUS 2019*,
https://doi.org/10.1007/978-3-030-29956-9_7

at evidentiary hearings in which guilt is grounded in the lower standard of "a preponderance of the evidence" (more likely than not to be true). In this sense, what happened to Haymond is a common occurrence. Indeed, this is the reason that the four dissenting Justices in *Haymond* were so worried about the decision's implications. If the reasoning behind the decision is taken to its logical conclusion, they warned, the "whole system of supervised release would be like a 40-ton truck speeding down a steep mountain road with no brakes."[1]

So, why did the Court overturn the sentence that Haymond received after his evidentiary hearing? And why did the dissenters warn that the decision places a major part of the criminal justice system in jeopardy? In addressing these questions, we must first briefly consider changes in criminal justice since the Founding which have raised difficult questions about how to square the goals of punishment—including the prevention of future crime—with the requirements of the Constitution.

The Historical Background of Supervised Release

The right to a jury trial is one of the most cherished rights in the Constitution. The Sixth Amendment guarantees that the accused in "all criminal prosecutions shall enjoy the right to a speedy and public trial, by an impartial jury…" This right embodies a commitment to liberty and self-government. No exercise of government power more immediately restricts individual liberty than a prosecution resulting in imprisonment. One of the ways that the Constitution sets bounds on the exercise of that power is by placing the judgment of the people—in the form of a jury verdict—between the government and the individual charged with a crime. Moreover, it has long been understood that the government can only secure a criminal conviction by proving its case to the jury "beyond a reasonable doubt," a requirement reflecting the belief that it is worse to imprison an innocent person than to let a guilty one remain free.[2]

---

[1] *Haymond* Alito dissent, page 9.
[2] *In re Winship*, 397 U.S. 358 (1970), Harlan concurrence, page 372.

While the vital importance of the right to a jury trial is widely recognized, many questions about its meaning are controversial. The issue at the heart of *U.S. v. Haymond* is when the right to a jury trial comes into play. While the Sixth Amendment states that the guarantee of a jury trial applies in all "criminal prosecutions," the meaning of that phrase today is far from obvious. The question was not always so complicated. In the period shortly after the Constitution's ratification, people predominantly thought that the purpose of punishment was retribution: to mete out the penalty that the criminal deserved based on the offense committed. The implementation of punishments was tied tightly to the crime committed, and determining when the jury right applied was relatively straightforward. "Criminal prosecution" was the stage where the government brought formal accusations against the defendant. By the end of the nineteenth century, however, the prevailing view was that punishment should aim to rehabilitate criminals, reforming their character and reintegrating them into society. A rehabilitative view focuses attention on each perpetrator's personal development after prison time begins. The treatment of offenders is individualized to their behavior following imposition of the sentence. With rehabilitative aims in mind, Congress adopted a parole system for federal crimes in 1910, and every state had adopted some form of it by the middle of the century. In the parole system, defendants were eligible for early release from prison depending on their behavior. Individuals released early—"parolees"—enjoyed conditional liberty for the remainder of the sentence. If parolees violated the conditions of release, they could be re-imprisoned for all or part of the time remaining from the initial sentence. The determination of whether to revoke parole and re-imprison an individual was made by a parole board, an agency of the prison system.[3]

The shift to a parole system raised questions about the scope of the jury right. Parolees were not afforded the usual protections of a criminal trial when the government sought to re-imprison them. Parole boards,

---

[3]Robert McClendon, "Supervising Supervised Release: Where the Courts Went Wrong on Revocation and How *U.S. v. Haymond* Finally Got It Right," 54 *Tulsa Law Review* 175 (2018), pages 180–181.

however, were nonetheless rendering judgments about how much time an individual would spend in prison based on whether they had committed certain alleged offenses. In concluding that parole board determinations did not violate the jury right, the Supreme Court drew a distinction between the *imposition* and the *administration* of a sentence. Imposition of the sentence—rendered by the court following conviction—was subject to the jury right. The sentence issued by the court upon conviction would set the bounds of possible prison time: the earliest eligibility for release and the maximum possible term. Within those bounds, parole boards could adjudicate revocation hearings—without affording the right to a jury trial—because they were merely administering the sentence that had been issued by the court with the assent of a jury. Thus, when parole boards re-imprisoned individuals on parole, they were not imposing a new or longer punishment; they were withdrawing the privilege of early release, which the parolee's behavior had shown they did not merit.[4]

Congress's replacement of parole with supervised release in the mid-1980s was designed to rectify perceived shortcomings in the former system. Parole fostered excessive uncertainty regarding the time offenders would serve in prison. It also unnecessarily yoked the period of supervision to the length of the prison term; no matter how well parolees progressed they had to be supervised for the entirety of the initial sentence. In addition, many thought that individuals subject to conditional liberty should be overseen by the judiciary rather than a branch of the prison system. The central change in supervised release concerns the relation between the completion of the sentence and the period of conditional liberty. A parolee was released *before* completing the sentence, and the period of supervision lasted for the time remaining on that sentence. In supervised release, the defendant is subject to a period of conditional liberty *after* completing the prison term imposed at the time of sentencing (with, perhaps, a small reduction for good behavior). Thus, the sentence imposed by a judge following conviction includes a prison term, to be followed by a period of supervised release.

---

[4]*Morrissey v. Brewer*, 408 U.S. 471 (1972) at 480.

The new system also moved oversight of released individuals to the judiciary. Notwithstanding these changes, supervised release retains a core idea of parole. In both systems, after serving time, individuals are subject to a period of conditional liberty during which they may be re-imprisoned for violating the requirements of release. Moreover, as in the revocation of parole, the government need not demonstrate guilt beyond a reasonable doubt to a jury. The determination is made by a judge, and the government must only establish its case by a preponderance of the evidence.[5]

The *Haymond* Decision: Three Opinions, Three Approaches

Let us return now to Andre Haymond. After a jury found him guilty of possessing child pornography, Haymond was sentenced to 38 months in prison to be followed by five years of supervised release. During the period of supervised release, the government sought Haymond's re-imprisonment, alleging that he was again in possession of child pornography. After an evidentiary hearing, the judge found for the government and sentenced Haymond to a five-year term of re-imprisonment. On appeal, Haymond challenged the constitutionality of a particular statutory provision that had influenced his sentence: § 3583(k) of the federal criminal code. In the absence of the challenged provision, the judge would have been authorized to re-imprison Haymond for a term between zero and two years. In 2006, however, as part of the Adam Walsh Child Protection and Safety Act, Congress enacted § 3583(k), requiring the judge in a case like Haymond's to impose a term of at least five years (and up to a term of life). The provision applies in cases where an individual who is required to register as a sex offender commits a crime punishable by more than one year in prison. Haymond claimed that § 3583(k) violated the Sixth Amendment by subjecting him to a new sentence without a jury trial.

---

[5]McClendon, "Supervising Supervised Release," page 182.

While people tend to overestimate the number of Supreme Court cases decided by a 5-4 margin, *Haymond* is just the kind of closely contested decision that many associate with the Court. The Justices issued three opinions. One opinion spoke for four Justices who voted strongly in favor of Haymond, and another spoke for four Justices who voted strongly against Haymond's position. As the deciding vote, Justice Breyer wrote an opinion siding with Haymond but largely agreeing with the reasoning of the Justices who voted against him. No wonder Supreme Court cases can be difficult to decipher!

When the Court splinters in this way, all of the opinions bear on the case's implications. As its position is the most clear-cut, we begin with the opinion that Justice Alito wrote for himself and the other three dissenting Justices (Chief Justice Roberts, and Justices Thomas and Kavanaugh). A critical question raised by *Haymond* is: "Does the jury right apply to the revocation of supervised release?" The dissent's answer is simply that the jury right does not apply in this context. In the dissent's view, a criminal prosecution ends when a defendant is sentenced following a jury conviction. If the sentence includes a period of supervised release, then any punishment that follows in connection with the supervised release must be understood as part of the initial sentence. We can see, then, why *Haymond* was an easy case for the dissenters. In their view, when the judge sentenced Haymond to a mandatory minimum sentence of five years under § 3583(k), he did not impose a new punishment. The five-year term was an outgrowth of the supervised release to which Haymond was sentenced after his jury trial. It was, therefore, also part of the initial sentence. Supporting their claim to have precedent on their side, the dissenters contended that supervised release is essentially the same as parole. This is critical, since the Court decided long ago that the government could revoke parole without a jury trial. For the dissenters, there is no constitutionally relevant distinction between a parolee released after five years of a ten-year sentence, on the one hand, and an individual subject to five years of supervised release after completing a five-year prison sentence, on the other. In either case, they stressed, the period of conditional liberty does not come with the same procedural protections enjoyed by individuals who were never convicted of a crime in the first place.[6]

The plurality opinion written by Justice Gorsuch for himself and Justices Ginsburg, Sotomayor, and Kagan, advances a fundamentally different approach to what counts as a criminal prosecution under the Sixth Amendment. For the plurality, the decisive consideration is the scope of the punishment authorized by a jury's verdict, namely the range of penalties available to the judge at the initial sentencing. Upon his conviction, Haymond was subject to a term of prison between zero and ten years. However, when he walked into his revocation hearing, Haymond faced the possibility of a sentence from five years to life. In the plurality's view, therefore, it was unconstitutional to subject Haymond to this new and more severe sentence without affording him the right to a jury trial.[7] Unlike the dissent, the plurality opinion viewed parole and supervised release as essentially distinct. A parolee was never subject to a greater sentence than what the jury authorized. Individuals on supervised release, by contrast, may end up serving much more time in prison than the sentence authorized by their initial conviction.[8]

While Justice Breyer largely agreed with the dissent's approach, he nevertheless deemed § 3583(k) unconstitutional. He identified two key problems with the provision's mandatory minimum sentence: it picks out specific crimes that trigger its application, and it interferes with judicial discretion. But why should these features matter? The acceptance of re-imprisonment without jury trials has depended on a rehabilitative conception of conditional liberty. The goal of overseeing individuals conditionally released from prison is to reform and reintegrate them into society. When individuals violate the conditions of release, they breach the trust that was placed in them. Re-imprisonment constitutes a response to that breach of trust, not a new punishment for the commission of a particular crime. Conceiving of supervised release

---

[6]*Haymond* Alito dissent, pages 9–17.
[7]*Haymond* Gorsuch plurality, pages 9–11.
[8]Ibid., page 17.

in this manner suggests that re-imprisonment amounts to the administration of an existing sentence rather than the imposition of a new one. We can best understand Justice Breyer's opinion as expressing the view that § 3583(k) cannot be made to plausibly fit with this model. A rehabilitative framework depends on the judge holding discretion to fit consequences to a particular defendant's situation, rather than imposing mandatory sentences (which raised objections even from the judge in Haymond's case). Moreover, § 3583(k)'s selection of particular crimes for mandatory minimum punishments suggests that its real focus is not so much on rehabilitation as it is on punishing crimes seen as presenting an especially pressing societal problem. It is notable in this respect that the provision challenged in *Haymond* was not enacted as part of a bill principally geared toward improving the system of supervised release. Rather, as stated in the legislation's preamble, the Adam Walsh Child Protection and Safety Act (of which 3583(k) is only a small part) was designed to "protect children from sexual exploitation and violent crime" and "to prevent child abuse and child pornography...."

The Decision's Implications

Haymond reinforces the significance of a single vote. If the dissenters had a fifth vote, Andre Haymond would be serving a five-year prison term, § 3583(k) would be constitutionally intact, and Congress would enjoy a green light to enact mandatory minimum sentences for specified crimes committed by individuals on supervised release. What if a fifth Justice had signed onto Justice Gorsuch's opinion, converting it from a plurality opinion into a majority opinion? This, too, would have momentous implications. Only propositions supported by a majority of the Justices have binding effect. With a fifth justice on board, Justice Gorsuch's opinion would speak with full legal authority. This might seem beside the point since Justice Breyer voted with Haymond in any event. It is true that Haymond's additional sentence was invalidated even without a fifth justice adding a signature to Justice's Gorsuch's opinion. Recall, however, that the plurality advocated a very different approach from the one espoused by Justice Breyer. The plurality's focus on the sentence range authorized by the jury's verdict implies constitutional difficulties with supervised release beyond § 3583(k)'s mandatory minimum. After all, there are many ways in the existing system that someone on supervised release could end up serving an overall period of time in prison longer than the range available to the judge at the initial sentencing. Moreover, the plurality opinion contains language suggesting that it may not just be the length of sentence that violates the Constitution, but the lack of a jury and a high standard of evidence for *any* impositions of additional prison time during supervised release. There might be far-reaching constitutional problems with the system of supervised release if the view of four current Justices is embraced by one more. It is just these suggestions that so alarm the dissenting Justices.[9]

For now, however, the legal force of any broader suggestions in the plurality opinion is blocked by Justice Breyer's opinion. In the short term, the terrain is largely controlled by Justice Breyer's pivotal vote. In this light, lawmakers would be wise to avoid drafting provisions that make it hard to keep a straight face while saying that the re-imprisonment of an individual on supervised release is really nothing more than a tweaking of the initial sentence.

The sharply divided vote in *Haymond* cannot help but bring to mind the impact of presidential politics on the Court's composition. In appointing Justices (with the Senate's approval), presidents hope to move the Court's decisions in a direction seen as favorable by the administration. Consequently, appointments often emerge as an issue in presidential campaigns. However, *Haymond* also emphasizes the unpredictability of the Justices' decisions. One might have expected Justice Gorsuch—appointed by Republican President Donald Trump—to vote with the four dissenting Justices, who were also appointed by Republicans. Instead, he joined three appointees of Democratic presidents. Indeed, Gorsuch has on numerous occasions allied with Justices generally thought of as liberal, particularly in criminal rights cases.

---

[9] *Haymond* Alito dissent, pages 1–9.

Thus, while presidential politics is critical to the makeup of the Court, there is no guarantee that a Justice will vote as anticipated.

Apart from the details of any particular piece of legislation, *Haymond* calls attention to a tension in criminal justice that has been present since the shift to a rehabilitative view of punishment. Rehabilitation requires individualized treatment, which, in turn, requires that someone determine the consequences of an offender's conduct. Flexibility and practicality demand streamlined procedures, but the Sixth Amendment demands the cumbersome protections of a jury trial. There is an underlying philosophical question here. No one doubts that a criminal conviction results in a loss of liberty. But what should we think about subjecting individuals to extended periods in which they do not enjoy the normal procedural protections? Should this be viewed as a natural and foreseeable consequence of committing crimes? Or might this intermediate status of legal protection raise constitutional difficulties? These questions have concrete ramifications. The requirements of a jury trial make it much more difficult to establish guilt. Indeed, the judge at Haymond's evidentiary hearing stated that if "this were a criminal trial and the Court were the jury, the United States would have lost."[10] The *Haymond* controversy highlights both stakes and challenges involved in attempting to reconcile the goals of punishment with the protections of the Constitution.

---

[10]Haymond's Brief to Supreme Court, page 7.

8

Kisor v. Wilkie on Deference to Federal Agencies

Bethany Blackstone

At first glance, *Kisor v. Wilkie* seems unlike many of the cases in this volume. The case is technical and does not involve the civil rights or civil liberties issues that most easily capture the public's interest. The case arose in a dispute surrounding James Kisor's efforts to obtain disability benefits from the Department of Veterans Affairs (VA). Mr. Kisor sought benefits for combat-related post-traumatic stress disorder (PTSD) associated with his service in Vietnam. His initial appeal, filed in 1982, was denied because Kisor could not show a clear diagnosis. In 2006, with a verified diagnosis of PTSD, he moved to reopen the claim and was awarded benefits from the date of his motion to reopen. However, Kisor argued that he should receive benefits from the date of his earlier request, grounded in "relevant" new evidence from his service record. The VA, however, concluded that Kisor's service records were not "relevant" under an applicable VA regulation. The case hinges on a core question about the law of administrative agencies: Who has the power to define the meaning of terms and concepts in government regulations?

B. Blackstone (✉)
University of North Texas, Denton, TX, USA
e-mail: Bethany.Blackstone@unt.edu

© The Author(s) 2020
D. Klein and M. Marietta (eds.), *SCOTUS 2019*,
https://doi.org/10.1007/978-3-030-29956-9_8

The Board of Veterans Appeals affirmed the agency's decision and Kisor appealed. The Court of Appeals for the Federal Circuit relied on the doctrine announced in *Auer v. Robbins*[1] and deferred to the agency's interpretation of the word "relevant" in the applicable regulation. *Auer* deference holds that when an agency's regulation is ambiguous, courts should defer to the agency's interpretation of the regulation's meaning as long as that interpretation is reasonable. Kisor asked the Supreme Court to reverse *Auer* and its predecessor *Bowles v. Seminole Rock & Sand Co.*[2]

Court observers have watched this case closely, not because of an abiding concern for the effective date of Mr. Kisor's benefits, but because federal agencies play a significant role in contemporary American policymaking across a wide range of issues. While liberals often look to federal agencies to implement progressive regulations of economic and social relations, a growing conservative legal movement calls for reigning in the federal bureaucracy. Those wary of the administrative state's power contend that the exercise of rulemaking power by unelected bureaucrats is in tension with the ideals of representative government; they argue that federal courts should ensure the primacy of legislative power by constraining agency action.[3] Courts can play this role because agency actions are subject to judicial review. A series of Supreme Court decisions that includes *Auer* guides federal judges in resolving disputes about agency interpretations of statutes and regulations. These cases articulate how deferential courts should be toward agency interpretations. More deferential standards increase agency power to shape policy while less deferential standards increase the policymaking role of courts. *Auer* deference has "become a target for conservatives and business groups, who believe it gives federal agencies too much power."[4]

---

[1]519 U.S. 42 (1997).

[2]325 U.S. 40 (1945).

[3]See, for example, Peter J. Wallison, *Judicial Fortitude: The Last Chance to Rein in the Administrative State* (New York: Encounter Books, 2018).

[4]Amy Howe, "Justices to Tackle Important Agency-Deference Question: In Plain English," SCOTUSblog, 28 January 2019.

The Court granted certiorari to consider overruling *Auer*. Many have looked to the case for insight into individual Justices' willingness to support overruling the Court's prior decisions. The debate about how deeply the Court should respect its prior rulings will influence a range of future controversies. Liberals are anxious to find out whether recent membership changes on the Supreme Court will result in the Court revisiting and reversing landmark liberal precedents, including *Roe v. Wade*[5] recognizing a woman's right to terminate a pregnancy by abortion prior to fetal viability.

On June 26, 2019, a five-justice majority declined to overrule *Auer*. Justice Kagan wrote the majority opinion for herself, Chief Justice Roberts, and Justices Ginsburg, Breyer, and Sotomayor. Kagan suggests the majority does little more than collect and review the Court's previously articulated limits on the applicability and use of *Auer* deference. Justice Gorsuch says that while claiming to adhere to *stare decisis*, the majority fundamentally reshapes the *Auer* doctrine.

Agency Rulemaking, the Administrative Procedure Act, and Deference

Understanding the Court's decision in *Kisor* requires some familiarity with the mechanisms agencies use to shape policy and their relationship to different forms of deference. Congress empowers agencies to promulgate rules that carry laws into effect. This practice allows those with subject-matter expertise to fill in the gaps left by legislation and to resolve ambiguities about the meaning of statutory language that arise in the course of implementing laws. To be clear, *Kisor v. Wilkie* involves an agency interpretation of one of its own regulations, not a statute. Even so, the logic of *Auer* and the arguments for overruling it are easier to understand when the case is situated alongside the Court's rules governing agency interpretation of statutes.

---

[5]410 U.S. 113 (1973).

Agencies with rulemaking authority can issue regulations that have the force of law. For example, to carry out a statutory directive to maintain a National Register of Historic Places, the National Park Service creates and enforces regulations that govern the listing of properties in the national register. The National Park Service recently proposed a rule that would prevent a proposed historic district from being listed in the National Register of Historic Places if the owners of a majority of the land at issue object to its inclusion.[6] This is an example of a *legislative rule* or a *substantive rule*.

Under the Administrative Procedure Act of 1946, most legislative rules must be promulgated via *notice-and-comment rulemaking*. This approach to rulemaking is designed to provide interested parties opportunities to participate in the rulemaking process. Agencies must publicly announce their intention to propose a new rule or to change existing rules and provide a mechanism for interested persons to provide comments on the proposed regulation. The agency must then review the submitted comments and respond to "significant" comments. Agencies may revise proposed regulations in response to comments received through this process.

Agencies can also adopt *interpretive rules* that "reflect an agency's construction of a statute that has been entrusted to the agency to administer."[7] The key distinction between *legislative rules* and *interpretive rules* is that the latter do not "bind" the public. That is, they cannot provide an independent basis for imposing rights and obligations on any person outside the agency.[8] Interpretive rules allow agencies to clarify their interpretations of ambiguous statutory or regulatory language in an expeditious manner. Since these rules do not create or alter existing substantive rights, agencies are not required to follow notice-and-comment procedures when they create them.

---

[6]National Register of Historic Places, 84 *Federal Register* 6996 (proposed March 1, 2019).

[7]Definition summarized in *Syncor International Corp. v. Shalala*, 127 F.3d 90 (D.C. Circuit 1997).

[8]Robert A. Anthony, "Interpretive Rules, Policy Statements, Guidances, Manuals and the Like—Should Federal Agencies Use Them to Bind the Public?" 41(6) *Duke Law Journal* 1311–1384 (1992).

Agency power to issue rules is subject to judicial review. The nature of a challenged agency action and the manner in which it was imposed will determine how deferential courts will be to the agency. The Supreme Court's decisions in *Chevron U.S.A., Inc. v. Natural Resources Defense Council, Inc.*[9] and *Skidmore v. Swift & Co.*[10] articulate two key deference regimes.

Chevron deference applies to an agency's challenged statutory interpretation if Congress delegated the agency authority to administer the statute being construed and the rule was promulgated through sufficiently formal procedures. Use of notice-and-comment rulemaking is the primary mechanism by which agencies secure *Chevron deference.* Even under *Chevron*, agency interpretations are not accepted blindly. If *Chevron* applies, courts undertake a two-step analysis. First, courts ask whether the statute is silent or ambiguous on the relevant issue. If Congress has spoken clearly, the agency's interpretation does not receive deference and Congress' policy prevails. If the statute is silent or ambiguous, courts defer to the agency's interpretation as long as it is reasonable. Importantly, courts are expected to employ all available tools of statutory construction before concluding that a statute is silent or ambiguous.

Chevron is a more deferential standard than its primary alternative—*Skidmore deference. Skidmore* tells judges to defer to agency interpretations only to the extent that they are persuasive. Among the factors that would increase the persuasiveness of an agency's interpretation are its cogency, its dependence on the agency's expertise, and reliance interests generated by long-standing agency constructions.

Critics of *Auer* deference contend that it is inconsistent with the logic of the Supreme Court's approach to deference because it muddies the distinction between *legislative* and *interpretive* rules. They characterize *Auer* as granting agency interpretations of regulations a level of deference that exceeds that in *Chevron*, without the associated procedural safeguards. Kisor calls on the Court to overrule *Auer* and to subject

---

[9]468 U.S. 837 (1984).
[10]323 U.S. 134 (1944).

agency interpretations of their ambiguous regulations to *Skidmore deference*. As respondent, the US government asks the Court to retain the core of *Auer* but to limit it by articulating a series of prerequisites that must be met before it is applied.

Auer Survives: "Potent in Its Place, but Cabined in Its Scope"

The *Kisor* majority writes that agency interpretations of their regulations are only entitled to *Auer deference* when three conditions are met: Genuine ambiguity remains after applying standard tools of interpretation; the agency's interpretation is reasonable; and the judgment is based on an agency's fair or considered judgment grounded in authoritative expertise. The majority says their approach is consistent with the Court's previously announced limits on *Auer* and that *stare decisis* cuts against overruling. However, the Justices split 4-4 on some of the key arguments advanced by Mr. Kisor. Four Justices take the position that *Auer* is inconsistent with the APA and that it violates the separation of powers, while four Justices reject those arguments; Chief Justice Roberts joins most of the majority opinion and endorses its conclusion, but refuses to join some parts of the argument, leaving his position unclear.

Justice Kagan writes that *Auer* deference is rooted in a presumption that Congress would generally prefer that agencies, rather than courts, play the primary role in resolving regulatory ambiguities. This presumption is based on four advantages of agency interpretations relative to judicial ones. First, agencies may have unique insight into what a challenged rule was intended to mean. Second, agencies may have scientific or technical expertise relevant to resolving regulatory ambiguities. Third, agencies are subject to more political accountability than federal judges. Fourth, deference to agency interpretations promotes uniformity, where resolution by courts may lead to conflict and uncertainty as lower courts reach differing conclusions on the best interpretation of an ambiguous regulation. This portion of the opinion is not joined by Chief Justice Roberts and only garners the support of four Justices so its precedential effect is ambiguous.

In the next section, Justice Kagan articulates limits on the applicability of *Auer*. Here, she writes for a majority of Justices including Roberts and says the opinion restates, clarifies, and clears up mixed messages the Court has sent regarding the applicability of *Auer* deference. Kagan acknowledges that the Court has sometimes applied *Auer* deference reflexively, without significant analysis of the underlying regulation or the nature and context of the interpretation. This, the majority concludes, is inappropriate. Kagan writes that *Auer* deference is only appropriate when the reasons for the presumption that Congress prefers agencies resolve regulatory ambiguity clearly apply. Determining whether deference is appropriate requires courts to undertake a careful analysis of the circumstances surrounding the challenged regulation.

The majority opinion clarifies that courts should use all traditional tools of interpretation before concluding that a challenged regulation presents genuine ambiguity. Citing *Chevron*, the majority notes deference is *not* appropriate where a careful analysis of the text, structure, and purpose of a regulation can resolve an alleged ambiguity. Further, even if ambiguity remains, courts should only defer if the agency's interpretation is *reasonable*. Finally, courts should consider whether the reasons underlying a presumption in favor of the agency's interpretation hold. If the comparative advantages enjoyed by agencies relative to courts discussed above do not apply to the regulation, courts need not defer.

The opinion lists several considerations judges should take into account in determining whether the presumption holds. It is stronger when the agency's interpretation embodies an official, authoritative position than when the challenged action comes in ad hoc statements from mid-level officials. It is stronger when the agency's interpretation relies on its unique substantive expertise. Finally, the presumption can only hold for interpretations that reflect an agency's "fair and considered judgment." Critics of *Auer* contend that by promoting blind deference, it permits agencies to draft intentionally vague regulations and to change interpretations abruptly. The majority states that deference is typically not warranted for agency interpretations that conflict with earlier ones or that otherwise fail to provide notice to regulated parties.

Arguments for Overruling

Four Justices—Thomas, Alito, Gorsuch, and Kavanaugh—assert that *Auer* should be overruled. They say *Auer* is poorly reasoned and inconsistent with the Administrative Procedure Act and separation of powers principles. Justice Gorsuch writes the primary opinion supporting overruling. He offers two core arguments, one about the meaning of the governing federal law and the second about the separation of powers under the Constitution.

The Administrative Procedure Act: Justice Gorsuch writes that *Auer* deference is inconsistent with Section 706 of the APA which instructs courts to "decide all relevant questions of law" and to "determine the meaning or applicability of the terms of an agency action." Gorsuch notes that many experts read Section 706 to require de novo review (starting from the beginning without reference to the conclusions made by earlier decision-makers). He concludes that *Auer* deference cannot be reconciled with the APA's commands. Justice Kagan counters that while the APA empowers courts to "determine the meaning" of agency actions, it does not prescribe a specific *method* for this inquiry. She concludes that deferring to an agency's interpretation is an appropriate way for courts to exercise review under Section 706. While Kagan sees *Auer* as providing "meaningful judicial review" of agency rules, Gorsuch does not.

Gorsuch also asserts that *Auer* deference is inconsistent with the APA's requirement of notice-and-comment rulemaking for binding regulations. Gorsuch says that *Auer* "obliterates" the distinction between legislative and interpretive rules by requiring courts to treat agency interpretations as controlling regardless of the manner in which they were announced. In Gorsuch's view, a rule requiring deference to agency interpretations of their regulations allows agencies to modify substantive regulations without following prescribed notice-and-comment procedures. Kagan disputes this view, arguing that the distinction between binding rules and interpretive rules remains important and noting that the Supreme Court recently rejected the argument that interpretive rules given *Auer* deference have the force of law.[11] While a court may defer to an agency's interpretation of a regulation, that interpretation is never the underlying basis of an enforcement action because the agency must always rely on a rule that went through notice-and-comment.

The Separation of Powers: Justice Gorsuch argues that *Auer* deference violates separation of powers principles. He argues that *Auer* tells judges that they must adopt an agency's interpretation even if it is not the best reading of the regulation and thus grants agencies an improper form of control over the exercise of judicial power. Kagan's response to the separation of powers argument is brief. She notes that the Court has repeatedly accepted that even when agency activities take legislative and judicial forms, they are understood to be exercises of executive power and thus do not violate the separation of powers. Kagan also reiterates that the majority's limits on *Auer* ensure that agency actions are subject to meaningful judicial review and thus do not violate the separation of powers.

The dispute between Kagan and Gorsuch also reflects different emphases on *stare decisis*. Writing for the majority, Kagan notes that *Auer* is part of a long line of precedents and that deference to agency interpretations of ambiguous rules "pervades the whole corpus of administrative law."[12] She cautions that overruling *Auer* would create instability in many areas of law by casting doubt on settled constructions of rules. Finally, Kagan notes that Congress is free to amend the APA if it disapproves of *Auer* deference. The majority interprets the lack of a congressional response to *Auer* as evidence of congressional acceptance of the doctrine.

Justice Gorsuch's opinion criticizes the majority for "reshaping our precedent in new and experimental ways" while claiming to adhere to *stare decisis*.[13] He argues that there was never a persuasive rationale underlying *Auer* deference and that the majority's efforts to save *Auer* by overhauling it reveal that it is unworkable. Gorsuch concludes

---

[11]*Perez v. Mortgage Bankers Association*, 575 U.S. ____ (2015).

[12]*Kisor* decision, page 26.

[13]*Kisor* Gorsuch concurrence, page 33.

by arguing that *Auer* has not generated serious reliance interests of the kind that result when an established rule is known and individuals make plans in accord with it. On the contrary, deference to new or unanticipated agency interpretations can create uncertainty. For these reasons, he characterizes *Auer* as an interpretive methodology that should not be subject to the strongest form of *stare decisis* and suggests that the Court could overrule *Auer's* general deference framework.

The Impact of the Decision

Justice Gorsuch's opinion characterizes the majority's version of *Auer* deference as "zombified" and as a "paper tiger."[14] While his opinion is highly critical of Justice Kagan's, Chief Justice Roberts and Justice Kavanaugh suggest the practical distance between the opinions is not so great. Each writes separately to emphasize that while *Kisor* articulates a more deferential standard than *Skidmore*, incorporating the limiting criteria enunciated in the decision ensures that the cases where deference applies will typically be those where even a court applying the more conservative standard of *Skidmore* would have come to the same conclusion that the agency's interpretation was reasonable.[15] In short, the policy implication of the Court's decision in *Kisor* is that courts will consistently undertake more rigorous review of agency interpretations of their regulations and, as a result, fewer should receive deference. *Auer* deference was maintained but limited.

Many anticipated the Court's conservative Justices would seize the opportunity to overrule *Auer* (and perhaps also the broader deference to administrative agencies under *Chevron*). Prior to the Court's grant of certiorari in *Kisor*, Chief Justice Roberts and Justices Alito, Thomas, and Gorsuch had expressed skepticism about *Auer's* continued vitality. Justice Roberts voting with the Court's four liberal Justices to uphold

---

[14]Ibid., pages 2, 3.

[15]*Kisor* Roberts concurrence, page 2; Kavanaugh concurrence, page 2.

the doctrine on the basis of *stare decisis* leaves *Auer* deference in place. While Kisor and his supporters hoped the Court would abandon *Auer*, the Justices leave open the possibility of revisiting this and other questions related to judicial review of agency actions. For example, Justices Roberts and Kavanaugh each write separately to highlight that the Court's decision in *Kisor* does not touch on questions related to agency interpretations of statutes. Ronald Levin characterizes the Court as choosing evolution rather than revolution and suggests that *Kisor* portends a continual, incremental approach to changes to the Court's rules governing deference.[16] *Kisor* does little to resolve questions about the future of established Supreme Court precedents. All Supreme Court Justices are willing to overrule *some* Supreme Court precedents and the ideological division on the Supreme Court ensures that, as in *Kisor*, the survival of some precedents will be sharply contested.

As for Mr. Kisor, his case returns to the Federal Circuit where judges will assess whether the VA's interpretation is one that Congress would want to receive deference, in accord with the guidelines articulated in *Kisor*. Regardless of the answer to that question, the large number of agency interpretations of regulatory and statutory language, combined with the Justices' continued interest in issues related to separation of powers, delegation, and deference ensure that the Court will continue to review and refine the rules that govern the relationship between executive branch agencies and federal courts.

---

[16]Ronald Levin, "*Auer* Deference—Supreme Court Chooses Evolution, Not Revolution," SCOTUSblog, 27 June 2019.

9

Madison, Bucklew, Dunn, and *Murphy* on Capital Punishment at the Margins

Mark A. Graber

The Supreme Court during the 2018–2019 term resolved four cases at the margins of disputes over the constitutionality of the death penalty. The substantive constitutional issues in the four cases—*Madison v. Alabama, Bucklew v. Precythe, Dunn v. Ray,* and *Murphy v. Collier*—concerned either when a person can become constitutionally ineligible for execution or the process by which condemned persons are executed, rather than more controversial issues concerning what crimes can be punished by death, what persons can be sentenced to death, or the process by which courts may determine whether a person has committed a death-eligible crime. The facts of each case were relatively unusual. The main case decided by the Supreme Court, *Madison v. Alabama,* revolved around whether Alabama courts had adequately considered a condemned person's dementia. *Bucklew v. Precythe* concerned a death-sentenced petitioner who claimed that the state method of execution by lethal injection would cause him unconstitutional pain because he suffered from an extremely rare medical condition. The other two

M. A. Graber (✉)
University of Maryland School of Law, Baltimore, MD, USA
e-mail: mgraber@law.umaryland.edu

© The Author(s) 2020
D. Klein and M. Marietta (eds.), *SCOTUS 2019,*
https://doi.org/10.1007/978-3-030-29956-9_9

cases to attract notice, *Dunn v. Ray* and *Murphy v. Collier*, concerned claims by condemned prisoners that states were discriminating against their religion by permitting spiritual advisors of some faiths to enter the execution chamber, but not a spiritual advisor of their faith. *Madison* was a dispute over the holding of a particular Alabama decision. The odds on the precise facts of *Bucklew* recurring, given the infrequency of executions, the few states that use lethal injections to execute, and the extreme rarity of Bucklew's medical condition, are close to infinitesimal. Given the low percentage of Muslims and Buddhists on death row and the willingness of almost all states to accommodate religious concerns when doing so is necessary to ensure an execution, the issues raised in the *Ray* and *Murphy* cases are almost as unlikely to recur. Whether the Supreme Court would have bothered deciding analogous cases that did not involve capital punishment is doubtful.

The more controversial issues concerning capital punishment nevertheless loomed large in all four cases. Madison had been on death row for more than three decades. Bucklew had been litigating the constitutionality of his sentence and means of execution for over twenty years. Ray and Murphy were asking for the Court to delay an imminent execution. The more conservative Justices on the Supreme Court, most notably Justices Neil Gorsuch and Samuel Alito, vigorously objected to how capital defense petitioners were able to delay their execution for decades, frequently making last-minute appeals to forestall their doom. The more liberal Justices on the Supreme Court, most notably Justices Stephen Breyer and Sonia Sotomayor, insisted that the Justices had obligations to offer capitally sentenced persons a robust appeals process that guaranteed deliberate resolution of all plausible constitutional claims, including last-minute appeals. The Justices seem to agree that the death penalty under contemporary constitutional rules is nearly impossible to implement, but conservatives think this means changing the constitutional rules, while liberals think this means abandoning capital punishment.

Madison v. Alabama

Vernon Madison was sentenced to death in 1985 for killing a police officer. During his very long stay on death row, his mental condition deteriorated. In 2016, Madison's lawyers filed a habeas corpus petition claiming he could not be executed because he lacked the mental capacity that such cases as *Ford v. Wainwright*[1] require for carrying out a death sentence. After a complex series of appeals, that claim was eventually denied. Madison filed a new claim of incompetence in 2018 after Alabama set an execution date. That claim maintained that he could not be constitutionally executed because his dementia had advanced to the point where he could no longer remember the crime for which he was capitally sentenced. A state trial court rejected that claim. Madison appealed to the Supreme Court of the United States.

By a 5-3 vote,[2] the Court remanded the case to the Alabama courts for further consideration grounded in the ruling. Justice Elena Kagan, writing for Chief Justice John Roberts and Justices Ginsburg, Sotomayor, and Breyer held that states could execute persons who did not remember their crimes, but not persons who do not understand why they are being executed. The critical question is whether a "prisoner's mental state is so distorted by a mental illness" that he lacks a "rational understanding" of "the State's rationale for [his] execution."[3] Memory loss could affect whether a prison had that rational understanding, but was not necessarily the decisive factor. "[I]f you somehow blacked out a crime you committed," Kagan pointed out, but later learned what you had done, you could well appreciate the State's desire to impose a penalty.[4] Kagan's opinion remanded the case because the majority believed the Alabama courts had not specifically focused on

---

[1] 477 U.S. 399 (1986).

[2] Justice Kavanaugh took no part in the ruling because he had not yet joined the Court when the case was argued on 2 October 2018.

[3] *Madison* decision, page 3.

[4] Ibid., page 10.

how dementia, as opposed to insanity, might make a death-sentenced person constitutionally ineligible for execution.

Justice Alito's dissent, joined by Justices Thomas and Gorsuch, did not dispute the majority's Eighth Amendment analysis, but claimed that the Court had not agreed when granting certiorari to consider whether dementia could make a prisoner execution ineligible. Alito added that the Alabama courts had adequately considered whether Madison's dementia made him unable to appreciate why he was being executed. Although the Alabama court spoke of insanity rather than dementia, Alito maintained that the context made clear that a "defendant suffers from 'insanity' if the prisoner does not understand the reason for his execution."[5]

Bucklew v. Precythe

Russell Bucklew in 1996 brutally murdered Michael Sanders, who was housing his estranged ex-girlfriend. Bucklew was convicted of murder by a Missouri trial court and sentenced to death. After failing to convince a series of appellate courts that he had been unconstitutionally sentenced to death, Bucklew challenged the process by which he was to be executed. Missouri by the mid-2010s had adopted lethal injection as the means for implementing the death penalty. Condemned prisoners were first injected with a sedative, pentobarbital, to prevent them from feeling any pain, and then given pancuronium bromide and potassium chloride, which induce paralysis and cardiac arrest. A divided Supreme Court in *Baze v. Rees*[6] and *Glossip v. Gross*[7] held that this method of execution did not violate the cruel and unusual punishment clause of the Eighth Amendment as incorporated by the Due Process Clause.[8]

---

[5]*Madison* Alito dissent, page 8.

[6]553 U.S. 35 (2008)

[7]576 U.S. ___ (2015).

[8]The Bill of Rights originally limited only the federal government. When a litigant claims a state law violates a provision of the Bill of Rights, they rely on the Due Process Clause of the Fourteenth Amendment ratified in 1868, which the Supreme Court in a series of cases has ruled

Bucklew then revised his challenge. His suit against Anne Precythe, the director of the Missouri Department of Corrections, claimed that Missouri's method of execution was unconstitutional as applied to him because he suffered from cavernous hemangioma, a rare disease that would prevent the sedative from adequately circulating in his body and result in the lethal injection causing excruciating and unconstitutional pain. The local federal district court and Court of Appeals for the Eighth Circuit rejected this claim. Bucklew appealed to the Supreme Court.

Bucklew's appeal highlights the difference between facial and as-applied challenges. Litigants challenge a law on its face when they maintain that the measure is unconstitutional in all circumstances. A law saying that no person may belong to a Christian church is facially unconstitutional; any government effort to prevent any person from belonging to a Christian church violates the Free Exercise Clause of the First Amendment. On the other hand, a law that requires persons to be vaccinated against certain contagious diseases is not facially unconstitutional. That law does not violate the constitutional rights of the vast majority of persons subject to vaccination.[9] Persons in particular circumstances, however, may claim that otherwise constitutional laws are nevertheless unconstitutional when applied in *their* circumstances. They make "as-applied" attacks on those measures. Some persons may suffer fatal allergic reactions if vaccinated. The vaccination law, therefore, may be unconstitutional as applied to them. Bucklew was making a similar as-applied claim. He was not asserting that Missouri could *never* use lethal injections to execute persons. That would be a facial attack. He was asserting that because of his rare medical condition, he would experience the sort of pain if given a lethal injection that violates the Eighth Amendment.

---

incorporates almost all of the provisions of the first eight amendments to the Constitution against state governments. (See the discussion of incorporation in Chapter 12.)

[9]See *Jacobson v. Massachusetts*, 197 U.S. 11 (1905).

Justice Gorsuch's majority opinion, which was joined by the other four more conservative members of the court, Chief Justice Roberts, Justice Alito, Justice Thomas, and Justice Brett Kavanaugh,[10] made relatively quick work of Bucklew's cruel and unusual punishment claim. Gorsuch began by pointing out that "The Constitution allows for capital punishment."[11] He noted that methods of execution, including hanging, accepted at the time of the Founding could be painful. From these observations, he drew the conclusion that while the Eighth Amendment prohibited "barbarous" executions, the Constitution "does not guarantee a prisoner a painless death."[12]

Gorsuch looked to *Baze v. Rees* for the standard that determines when an execution protocol causes unconstitutional pain. Government, he concluded, had to make reasonable efforts to select a relatively painless execution, but was not required to forego capital punishment should the risk of excruciating pain to a particular condemned person be relatively high. "A prisoner must show a feasible and readily implemented method of execution that would significantly reduce a substantial risk of severe pain," Gorsuch wrote, "and that the State has refused to adopt without a legitimate penological reason."[13] Put more simply, the punishment must "superadd pain well beyond what's needed to effectuate a death sentence."[14] Justice Clarence Thomas' concurring opinion further insisted that the punishment must be "deliberately designed to inflict pain."[15] Both Gorsuch and Thomas agreed that Bucklew did not meet this standard. Bucklew proposed that he be executed by nitrogen gas. The majority, however, claim that no evidence existed that execution by nitrogen gas was feasible or that execution by nitrogen gas would likely cause Bucklew substantially less pain.

---

[10]Kavanaugh also wrote a short concurring opinion on the availability of alternative methods of execution.

[11]*Bucklew* decision, page 8.

[12]Ibid., page 11.

[13]Ibid., page 13.

[14]Ibid., page 16.

[15]*Bucklew* Thomas concurrence, page 1.

Justice Breyer's dissent, joined by the other three more liberal members of court, Justices Ginsburg, Sotomayor, and Kagan, disputed the majority opinion's legal and factual conclusions. Breyer and the more liberal Justices in dissent insisted that the proper standard for determining whether an execution protocol was consistent with the Eighth Amendment was whether the method of imposing capital punishment caused horrible pain. While Gorsuch put the burden on the capitally sentenced prisoner to demonstrate an alternative, less painful method of execution, Breyer put the burden on the state to demonstrate that the execution protocol was likely to be painless. If a method of execution was "concededly torturous,"[16] he asserted, then the lack of an alternative method of execution was not constitutionally relevant. The dissent also claimed that Bucklew had presented substantial facts to support his as-applied challenge to Missouri's execution protocol. Breyer pointed out that several states had adopted nitrogen gas as a method of execution, suggesting the method was feasible. Moreover, he noted, Bucklew presented evidence in the lower federal courts, admittedly contested, that execution by nitrogen gas would be far less painful for him.

Potentially more consequential capital punishment issues were tucked away at the end of the majority opinion and Breyer's dissent, as well as throughout Sotomayor's separate dissent. Gorsuch concluded his opinion by complaining about how death-penalty lawyers were frustrating the capital punishment system by bringing last-minute appeals. "The people of Missouri, the surviving victims of Mr. Bucklew's crimes, and others like them deserve better," Gorsuch wrote, than a process that permitted Bucklew "to secure delay through lawsuit and lawsuit."[17] The Supreme Court, he indicated, needed to police the last-minute stay process more thoroughly. Gorsuch concluded, "Last-minute stays should be the extreme exception, not the norm, and the last-minute nature of an application that could have been brought earlier or an applicant's attempt at manipulation may be grounds for denial of a stay."[18] Breyer

---

[16]*Bucklew* Breyer dissent, page 14.
[17]*Bucklew* decision, page 29.
[18]Ibid., page 30.

agreed with Gorsuch that "Undue delays in death penalty cases frustrate the interests of the State and of surviving victims."[19] Nevertheless, he believed that constitutional values trumped the efficiency of the execution process. "It may be that there is no way to execute a prisoner quickly, while affording him the protections that our Constitution guarantees to those who have been singled out for our law's most severe sanction."[20] Sotomayor was more blunt. "There are higher values than ensuring that executions run on time," she wrote. In her view, "If a death sentence or the manner in which it is carried out violates the Constitution, that stain can never come out."[21]

Dunn v. Ray and Murphy v. Collier

Domineque Ray was scheduled to be executed on February 7, 2019, for a rape, robbery, and murder committed in 1995. Ten days before his execution, he filed a petition in the Eleventh Circuit claiming that Alabama was violating his constitutional rights by refusing to let a Muslim imam accompany him in the execution chamber. Alabama permitted death-sentenced persons to have a minister of their faith be with them in the hours leading up to the execution and then view the execution from another room, but only the chaplain employed by the prison, who had always been Christian, could be in the execution chamber. On January 23, 2019, Alabama refused Ray's request to have the minister of his choice in the chamber. Ray filed a petition asking for relief five days later. The Court of Appeals for the Eleventh Circuit granted a stay of execution to determine whether Alabama practice violated the Establishment Clause of the First Amendment as incorporated by the Due Process Clause of the Fourteenth Amendment. Alabama immediately asked the Supreme Court to reverse that decision and, in legal terms, "vacate" the stay.

---

[19] *Bucklew* Breyer dissent, page 16.
[20] Ibid., page 18.
[21] *Bucklew* Sotomayor dissent, page 5.

Patrick Murphy was scheduled to be executed on March 28, 2019, for the murder of a police officer in 2000. On March 20, 2019, Murphy filed a lawsuit against Bryan Collier, the executor director of the Texas Department of Justice, claiming a constitutional right to have a Buddhist priest accompany him in the execution chamber. Texas law (as in Alabama) permitted only clerics employed by the Department of Corrections to accompany the condemned person in the execution chamber. At the time, the Department of Corrections employed only Christian and Muslim clerics. Texas on March 5, 2019, informed Murphy and his counsel of the state policy, but the state did not respond when counsel asked whether the state employed any Buddhist clerics. Both the Texas Court of Criminal Appeals and the lower federal courts refused to issue a stay. Murphy appealed to the Supreme Court of the United States.

The Supreme Court by a 5-4 vote vacated the stay of execution in *Dunn v. Ray*, but by a 6-3 vote in *Murphy v. Collier* granted a stay of execution. The *Dunn* majority consisted of the five more conservative Justices, Chief Justice Roberts and Justices Kavanaugh, Alito, Thomas, and Gorsuch. They simply announced the stay was being vacated without issuing an opinion. Justice Kagan wrote a short dissent signed by the other liberals on the bench, Justices Ginsburg, Breyer, and Sotomayor. The *Murphy* majority consisted of the four liberals, plus Roberts and Kavanaugh. Kavanaugh wrote a short opinion for the majority and a somewhat longer opinion joined by Roberts, explaining what they perceived to be the differences between *Ray* and *Murphy*. Justice Alito wrote a dissent signed by Gorsuch and Thomas.

The judicial majority in *Murphy* agreed that unconstitutional religious discrimination occurs when states permit ministers of some faiths to accompany condemned persons in the execution chamber, but not ministers of other faiths. Justice Kavanaugh's opinion concurring in the stay grant argued that if Texas policy "allows a Christian or Muslim inmate to have a state-employed Christian or Muslim religious advisor present in either the execution room or in the adjacent viewing room," then Texas must allow other inmates to have the religious advisor of their choice in either the execution room or in the adjacent viewing room. The contrary practice was "denominational discrimination."[22] Justice Kagan's dissent in *Dunn v. Ray* pointed out that such discrimination must meet a high legal standard. The state must "show that its policy is narrowly tailored to a compelling interest."[23] Neither Alabama nor Texas could meet that burden. Neither offered substantial reasons why, if some ministers could enter the execution chamber, ministers of other faiths could not. Kavanaugh and Roberts justified their refusal to grant Ray relief in part because they believed Ray was not asking simply for equal treatment but for the right to have a cleric of his faith in the execution chamber. Alabama in response to Ray's petition, Kavanaugh wrote, had changed state practice so that no clerics of any faith were permitted in the execution chamber. For this reason, Kavanaugh asserted, Ray was no longer suffering unconstitutional discrimination.

Alito was less sure that Texas and Alabama were violating religious freedom rights. Government, he pointed out, often limits prisoner's rights when analogous limits outside of the prison would be unconstitutional. Religious freedom was no different. Alito's dissent in *Murphy* maintained that the standard for religious discrimination in a prison setting was lower than the standard for religious discrimination in other contexts. In the prison setting, he wrote, government must establish only: "(1) whether a prison rule bears a valid, rational connection to a legitimate governmental interest; (2) whether alternative means are open to inmates to exercise the asserted right; (3) what impact an accommodation of the right would have on guards, inmates, and prison resources; and (4) whether there are ready alternatives to the regulation."[24] Alito suggested that states might have a valid reason for allowing only trained clergy to accompany inmates in the execution chamber, as long as no religious discrimination existed in which clergy received the relevant training.

The more enduring issue in both *Ray* and *Murphy* was over the stays of execution. The three judicial opinions were fact-specific. Kavanaugh

---

[22]*Murphy* Kavanaugh concurrence, page 2.

[23]*Ray* Kagan dissent, page 2.

[24]*Murphy* Alito dissent, page 9.

split the difference. Murphy was entitled to a stay of execution because the delay was partly caused by Texas not responding to his question about whether the state employed a Buddhist cleric who could accompany him in the execution chamber. Ray was not entitled to a stay of execution because he made his request for an imam much closer to the execution date. Kagan maintained that Ray was entitled to a stay of execution because his request for an imam in his execution chamber was denied on January 23, 2019, and Ray's lawyers filed the appropriate lawsuit only five days later. Alito maintained Murphy was not entitled to a stay because Murphy was on death row when Texas adopted their execution protocol in 2013, should have filed his action in November 2018 when his execution date was set, or, at the very least, should have followed-up when Texas in March did not respond to his request for a Buddhist cleric in the execution chamber.

The Fraying of America's Death Penalty Compromises

Of the four cases this year, *Madison* may best illustrate the constitutional trench warfare that has occupied death-penalty lawyers for several decades, with each side fighting for very few feet of constitutional space. The other three cases—*Bucklew, Ray,* and *Murphy*—suggest that the explicit and implicit compromises that structured capital punishment in the United States for almost fifty years are weakening. The explicit compromise forged in the 1970s in such cases as *Gregg v. Georgia*[25] was that states could constitutionally impose capital punishment, but only if they adopted special procedures that would maximize accuracy and ensure race-neutral implementation of the death penalty. A very high percentage of death sentences imposed at trial do not survive these procedural hurdles. More often than not, years of appellate litigation demonstrates that death-sentenced prisoners were either not constitutionally eligible to be executed or that their trials suffered

---

[25]428 U.S. 153 (1976).

from constitutional flaws.[26] The implicit compromise is that the death penalty would exist in legal books, but hardly ever in practice. While conservatives blame death-penalty lawyers for dragging out the capital sentencing process, states are responsible for much of the delay. Prosecutors who obtain death verdicts are very slow to set execution dates, in part because the trial sentence suffices for their political goals and in part because they do not wish to spend the time and expense actually necessary to execute a condemned person.[27]

No Justice on the contemporary court seems happy with the explicit and implicit compromises of the past. Conservatives want to streamline the capital sentencing process in ways that will make executions cheaper and, they believe, more frequent. Liberals insist that the compromises of the past have demonstrated that no system of capital punishment can achieve constitutional standards for accuracy and fairness. Both Gorsuch and Breyer in *Bucklew* and other cases have declared their willingness to move the execution process away from the present uncomfortable middle. Gorsuch, however, is the Justice at present who likely has the majority support necessary to make his more extreme vision of the capital sentencing process the official constitutional law of the land.

---

[26]See James S. Liebman, et al., "Capital Attrition: Error Rates in Capital Cases, 1973–1995," 78 *Texas Law Review* (2000) 1839.

[27]See Carol S. Steiker and Jordan M. Steiker, *Courting Death: The Supreme Court and Capital Punishment* (Cambridge, MA: Harvard University Press, 2016); Lee Kovarsky, "The American Execution Queue," 71 *Stanford Law Review* 1163 (2019).

10

Mitchell v. Wisconsin on Blood Alcohol Tests Under the Fourth Amendment

Pamela C. Corley

This case began when a police officer received information that Gerald Mitchell was driving a van under the influence of alcohol. The officer found Mitchell wandering around a lake and gave him a preliminary breath test. Mitchell's blood alcohol content (BAC) was three times the legal limit and the officer arrested him for driving under the influence. However, on the way to the police station to take a more reliable test, Mitchell's condition became much worse so the officer took him to a hospital. By the time they arrived, Mitchell had passed out and a blood sample was taken while he was still unconscious. Those results showed that his BAC was .222% and based on that evidence he was subsequently charged with two drunk-driving offenses. Mitchell moved to suppress the blood alcohol test on the grounds that it was an unreasonable search under the Fourth Amendment because the police did not have a warrant. The trial court disagreed, Mitchell was convicted, and the Wisconsin Court of Appeals certified two questions to the Wisconsin Supreme Court: Whether Mitchell consented under

P. C. Corley (✉)
Southern Methodist University, University Park, TX, USA
e-mail: pccorley@smu.edu

© The Author(s) 2020
D. Klein and M. Marietta (eds.), *SCOTUS 2019*,
https://doi.org/10.1007/978-3-030-29956-9_10

the implied consent law and whether a warrantless blood test from an unconscious person violates the Fourth Amendment. The Wisconsin Supreme Court affirmed Mitchell's conviction and the US Supreme Court agreed to hear the case.

What are the police allowed to do when they suspect a person of driving under the influence? Can they require the person to submit to a breath test? A blood alcohol test? The Fourth Amendment protects against unreasonable searches and seizures, and the Supreme Court has held that a search by the government generally requires a warrant from a judge. However, there are many exceptions to the warrant requirement, including a search incident to arrest (which allows the police to search a person and the area within her immediate control after being lawfully arrested), the exigent circumstances exception (which permits a warrantless search to prevent the imminent destruction of evidence), and an exception if the person consents. Does the Fourth Amendment allow the police, without a warrant, to obtain a blood test from an unconscious driver who appears to have been driving under the influence of alcohol? This is the question the Court answered in *Mitchell v. Wisconsin*.

Under Wisconsin's implied consent law, a person driving on Wisconsin roads is deemed to have consented to having a breath or blood test if an officer reasonably believes they are driving drunk. A person can refuse, withdrawing her consent; however, if that happens, the person's license is revoked. The law further provides that if a person is unconscious, the presumption is that she has *not* withdrawn her consent, and the search can be undertaken. This controversy may seem to be a narrow one focused on drunk driving—and only on unconscious drivers at that—but civil liberties advocates see a broad range of implications if the state can invade a person's body based on implied consent. The American Civil Liberties Union filed an amicus brief, arguing that for consent to be truly voluntary, the person consenting must have the freedom to change her mind and, given that an unconscious person cannot make a choice at all, the person has not consented. Do people consent to a search whenever they do something as ordinary as walk down the street using a cell phone? *Mitchell* is indeed about drunk driving, but its principles may apply to much more.

The Plurality Opinion

In a plurality opinion that did not command a full majority of the Justices,[1] the Court decided that when a driver is unconscious and cannot be given a breath test, the exigent circumstances exception generally allows a blood test without a warrant. Justice Samuel Alito wrote the plurality opinion for only four Justices (joined by Chief Justice Roberts and Justices Breyer and Kavanaugh). Justice Thomas wrote an opinion concurring in judgment only, which means he agreed with the result that was reached, but not with the reasoning of the Court. Justice Sotomayor wrote a dissenting opinion, joined by Justices Ginsburg and Kagan. Justice Gorsuch also wrote a dissenting opinion.

The precedents on alcohol testing are somewhat nuanced but do not address the circumstances of an unconscious driver. The Court previously held in *Birchfield v. North Dakota* that in an arrest for drunk driving a warrantless *breath* test is allowed under the Fourth Amendment, but not a warrantless *blood* test.[2] The crucial distinction the Court noted is the degree of *intrusiveness*: Blood tests pierce the skin and take part of a person that can be maintained for future DNA tests. The Fourth Amendment protects bodily integrity more than it does simple searches. In *Missouri v. McNeely*, the Court decided that the mere fact that blood alcohol evidence dissipates rapidly does not allow the police to conduct a warrantless blood alcohol test under the exigent circumstances exception.[3] However, in *Schmerber v. California*, the Court allowed a warrantless blood test given that the defendant was taken to the hospital after a car accident and the officer had to stay on the accident scene to investigate; therefore, there was no time to get a warrant.[4]

The plurality opinion discussed the importance of blood alcohol testing given that "highway safety is a vital public interest," that BAC limits

---

[1]A plurality opinion is the controlling judgment when a majority of Justices agree on the outcome but *not* on the justification or reasoning; only a smaller number—the plurality—offer an opinion that explains the Court's position, which may limit the power of the ruling.

[2]*Birchfield v. North Dakota*, 579 U.S. ___ (2016).

[3]*Missouri v. McNeely*, 569 U.S. 141 (2013).

[4]*Schmerber v. California*, 383 U.S. 757 (1966).

contribute to highway safety, and that enforcing BAC limits requires a test that can be used in court.[5] Enforcing those limits requires "prompt testing because it is 'a biological certainty' that '[a]lcohol dissipates from the bloodstream at a rate of 0.01 percent to 0.025 percent per hour... Evidence is literally disappearing by the minute.'"[6] And for an unconscious driver, a blood test is necessary to achieve those compelling interests. Does this compelling need justify a warrantless search?

According to Justice Alito, Mitchell's medical condition was similar to the exigency situation the Court found in *Schmerber*. Mitchell's unconsciousness prevented the police from obtaining a more reliable breath test. But was a warrantless blood test reasonable? Alito acknowledged that a blood test is a search and thus a warrant is generally required; however, he recognized that the exigent circumstances exception allows a warrantless search when "there is compelling need for official action and no time to secure a search warrant."[7] Alito concluded that in general the exception applies to unconscious drivers: "In those cases, the need for a blood test is compelling, and an officer's duty to attend to more pressing needs may leave no time to seek a warrant."[8] In Mitchell's specific case, the plurality sent the proceedings back to the Wisconsin courts to allow Mitchell to make the argument that exigent circumstances may not have existed in his situation. But the principle of the exigent circumstances exception for unconscious drivers is now established.

Alito's plurality opinion noted that "even if the constant dissipation of BAC evidence *alone* does not create an exigency [which the Court decided in *McNeely*]...*Schmerber* shows that it does so when combined with other pressing needs."[9]

> Thus, exigency exists when (1) BAC evidence is dissipating and (2) some other factor creates pressing health, safety, or law enforcement needs that

---

[5]*Mitchell* decision, page 10.
[6]Ibid., page 11 (quoting *McNeely*, 169).
[7]Ibid., page 8 (quoting *McNeely*, 149).
[8]Ibid., page 9.
[9]Ibid., page 13.

would take priority over a warrant application. Both conditions are met when a drunk-driving suspect is unconscious, so *Schmerber* controls: With such suspects, too, a warrantless blood draw is lawful.[10]

According to the plurality, an unconscious drunk driver presents a medical emergency just like getting medical help for a drunk driver involved in a car accident. Both of these situations fall within the exigent circumstances exception because they involve pressing needs. Alito asserts that "in many unconscious-driver cases, the exigency will be *more* acute," not less.

> A driver so drunk as to lose consciousness is quite likely to crash, especially if he passes out before managing to park. And then the accident might give officers a slew of urgent tasks beyond that of securing (and working around) medical care for the suspect. Police may have to ensure that others who are injured receive prompt medical attention... provide first aid... deal with fatalities... preserve evidence... redirect traffic to prevent further accidents. These pressing matters, too, would require responsible officers to put off applying for a warrant, and that would only exacerbate the delay—and imprecision—of any subsequent BAC test.[11]

Finally, the plurality addressed Mitchell's argument that, given technological advances, warrants can be obtained very quickly and easily and thus, a warrantless blood test is unnecessary in the case of an unconscious driver. Although the plurality agreed that the time required has diminished, it still does take some time; thus, if police officers are forced to obtain a warrant in an emergency situation there could be "terrible collateral costs."[12] Thus, the Court held that if the police have probable cause to believe a person is guilty of drunk driving and that person is unconscious and has to go to the hospital, the police may "almost always" order a blood test without a warrant.[13]

---

[10]Ibid.
[11]Ibid., page 15.
[12]Ibid., page 16.
[13]Ibid.

Justice Thomas' Concurrence

Justice Thomas concurred in the result only, disagreeing with the reasoning of the Court. Thomas criticized the plurality for a "difficult-to-administer rule."[14] Instead, Thomas argued that the rule should be a simple one: The fact that alcohol naturally dissipates in the blood creates an exigent circumstance (specifically, the imminent destruction of evidence). Once police have probable cause to believe that a driver is drunk, it doesn't matter if the driver is unconscious or not. Basically, Thomas believes that *McNeely* was wrongly decided because exigency is paramount.

The Dissenters Respond

Justice Sotomayor wrote a dissenting opinion, which was joined by Justices Ginsburg and Kagan. According to the dissenters, if the police have time to get a warrant, they should get one. It is as simple as that.

The dissent pointed out that Wisconsin even conceded that there was no exigency in this case that would justify the warrantless blood test and instead argued based on its implied consent law. Sotomayor argued that Wisconsin waived the exigency issue and the Court should not have considered it.

In any event, the dissent did not believe there was any exigency based on previous case law and the facts of the case. Previous case law established that the exigent circumstances exception only applies if the State shows a "compelling need for official action and no time to secure a warrant."[15] The dissenters argued that "the fact that a suspect fell unconscious at some point before the blood draw does not mean that there was insufficient time to get a warrant."[16] And there is always delay in order to do a blood test because the police have to drive the

---

[14]*Mitchell* Thomas concurrence, page 1.
[15]*Mitchell* Sotomayor dissent, page 11.
[16]Ibid.

suspect to the medical facility and wait for medical personnel to draw the blood. According to the dissent, that built-in delay gives police time to get a warrant, especially given technological advances, and "a small delay to obtain a warrant is hardly a recipe for lawless roadways."[17] The dissent argued that *McNeely* rejected a categorical exigency exception for blood tests and the suspected drunk driver being unconscious doesn't change anything.

Justice Sotomayor and the other dissenters also disagreed with the plurality opinion's assumption that being unconscious leads to the need for urgent medical care. Even if that is true, that doesn't necessarily mean that there won't be time to get a warrant:

> Acting entirely on its own freewheeling instincts—with no briefing or decision below on the question—the plurality permits officers to order a blood draw of an unconscious person in all but the rarest cases, even when there is ample time to obtain a warrant. The plurality may believe it is helping to ameliorate the scourge of drunk driving, but what it really does is to strike another needless blow at the protections guaranteed by the Fourth Amendment. With respect, I dissent.[18]

Justice Gorsuch also dissented, disagreeing with the Court's decision not to answer the question presented, which was whether Mitchell consented under Wisconsin's implied consent law. Thus, Gorsuch believed that the Court should have dismissed the case as improvidently granted and waited for a case that squarely presented the exigent circumstances issue. Instead, the case had to be remanded back in order for the lower court to decide if there was an exigent circumstance in this case.

---

[17]Ibid., page 13.
[18]Ibid., page 18.

Conclusion

So what does all this mean? Four Justices agreed that police may order a warrantless blood test for an unconscious driver under the exigent circumstances exception to the warrant requirement. One Justice believed that police may order a warrantless blood test in any suspected drunk driving situation given that the alcohol in the blood naturally dissipates. Three Justices did not believe the exigent circumstances exception automatically covers unconscious suspected drunk drivers and one Justice did not explain whether the exigent circumstances exception applies, instead arguing that the case should have been dismissed.

There are still questions the Court has yet to answer. By driving on a state's roads, have you consented to a blood test, even if you are unconscious? The Supreme Court did not answer that question, which is an important one given that more than half the states have similar laws. These implied consent laws could be expanded to apply to other searches, such as cell phones and car black boxes.

Will Gerald Mitchell's blood test ultimately be able to be used against him? The Supreme Court did not answer that question, instead remanding the case to the Wisconsin Supreme Court. However, it does appear that the US Supreme Court has expanded the power of the police to conduct warrantless searches, at least with respect to unconscious drunk driving suspects. Although the Court did not decide that the fact that alcohol naturally dissipates in the blood creates an exigent circumstance, the Court did hold that being an unconscious drunk driver almost always creates an exigent circumstance that permits a warrantless blood test. By expanding what constitutes an exigent circumstance, the Court has diminished a person's privacy rights.

11

Rucho v. Common Cause on Partisan Gerrymandering and the Political Questions Doctrine

Carol Nackenoff and Abigail Diebold

When Massachusetts Governor Elbridge Gerry redrew his young state's electoral districts in 1812 in an attempt to advantage Jefferson's Democratic-Republicans over Hamilton's Federalists, a contemporary noted that one of the new districts resembled a salamander. The move was quickly dubbed a "Gerry-mander."[1] This term is now used to refer to any method of redistricting that privileges the votes of one group over another. When the Court heard oral arguments in *Rucho v. Common Cause* (decided with *Lamone v. Benisek*) in March of 2019, partisan redistricting already had a long history in American law and politics.

Rucho and *Lamone* concerned challenges to the constitutionality of congressional districts that were drawn to entrench the dominance of

---

[1]See the iconic cartoon of this 1812 district (sometimes attributed to Gilbert Stuart, though most likely penned by Elkanah Tisdale, with Richard Alsop supplying the term) at www.smithsonianmag.com/history/where-did-term-gerrymander-come.

C. Nackenoff (✉) · A. Diebold
Swarthmore College, Swarthmore, PA, USA
e-mail: cnacken1@swarthmore.edu

© The Author(s) 2020
D. Klein and M. Marietta (eds.), *SCOTUS 2019*,
https://doi.org/10.1007/978-3-030-29956-9_11

111

one political party. Proponents of the North Carolina and Maryland redistricting plans openly conceded that the explicit purpose of the mapping decisions was to gain partisan advantage in congressional elections.

In *Rucho*, North Carolina districts had been redrawn by the General Assembly to disadvantage Democratic voters following a Supreme Court decision in 2017 striking down the state's previous map as an unconstitutional racial gerrymander.[2] The Republican majority then redrew the map along *partisan* lines; one of the architects proposed to "draw the maps to give partisan advantage to 10 Republicans and three Democrats, because I do not believe it is possible to draw a map with 11 Republicans and two Democrats."[3] In 2018, despite receiving just 50.5% of the votes (to the Democrats' 48.3%), Republican congressional candidates took 10 of the 12 decided seats.[4]

Lamone presented a challenge to Maryland's sixth congressional district, where many voters were moved to create a new Democratic stronghold in redistricting following the 2010 census; voter shuffling split some counties for the first time in nearly two centuries. Although Republican congressional candidates received roughly one-third of the vote in 2018, Maryland Democrats, led by self-proclaimed "serial gerrymanderer" Congressman Steny Hoyer,[5] had constructed a congressional delegation reliably consisting of seven Democrats and one Republican.

Both *Rucho* and *Lamone* reached the Court as mandatory appeals under a federal statute[6] allowing parties in suits decided by a three-judge district court panel (including challenges to districting and apportionment) to appeal directly to the Supreme Court. This mandatory appeals process raised the stakes of the Court's decision: Without

---

[2]*Cooper v. Harris*, 581 U.S. ___ (2017).

[3]Ralph Hise and David Lewis, "We Drew Congressional Maps for Partisan Advantage. That Was the Point," *Atlantic*, 25 March 2019; Adam Liptak, "Partisan Gerrymander Returns to a Transformed Supreme Court," *The New York Times*, 18 March 2019.

[4]The Ninth District seat remained unfilled pending a special election slated for 10 September 2019.

[5]*Rucho* decision, page 6.

[6]USC 28 § 2284 (1940).

a clear answer to the question of partisan gerrymandering, the Court would continue to face an onslaught of appeals, particularly following the 2020 census.

The Court's decision would have serious repercussions beyond the specific states involved. The Court was being asked to decide whether partisan gerrymandering could ever be remedied by federal courts and, if so, under what standard.

The Political Questions Doctrine

Perhaps the strongest argument against Court intervention is the *political questions doctrine*, which established that the Court should refrain from ruling on matters that are beyond its judicial powers or are more properly dealt with by the electoral branches. Until the 1960s, the Court considered state malapportionment of legislative seats to be a political question.[7] In *Baker v. Carr* (1962)—the first time the Court intervened in a re-apportionment controversy to establish congressional districts of equal size under the Fourteenth Amendment's equal protection clause—Justice Brennan's majority opinion articulated several criteria for identifying a political question, including (1) if there is a clear, textual, constitutional commitment of an issue to another branch of the federal government; and (2) if the Court cannot find "judicially discoverable and manageable standards for resolving" a controversy. When the Court refrains from engagement because it cannot devise or identify appropriate tests or standards, it means that constitutional guarantees may not yield judicially enforceable rights.[8]

Justice Frankfurter, dissenting in *Baker*, warned the Court against involvement in controversies over the uneven number of persons

---

[7]In *Luther v. Borden*, 48 U.S. 1 (1849), the Court held that determining which of two Rhode Island governments met the republican form of government promise under Article IV §4 was a political question, to be resolved by the other branches.

[8]Richard J. Fallon, Jr., "Judicially Manageable Standards and Constitutional Meaning," 119 *Harvard Law Review* 1275–1332 (March 2006). See also Morgan Marietta, "Roberts Rules," *The Conversation* online, 8 July 2016.

in electoral districts. For him, "there is not under our Constitution a judicial remedy for every political mischief" and "courts ought not to enter this political thicket."[9]

However, after *Baker* the Court continued its involvement. Decisions in *Reynolds v. Sims* (1964) (concerning state legislative districts) and *Wesberry v. Sanders* (1964) (for US congressional districts) held that under the equal protection clause and Article I §2, electoral districts must be as equal in population as possible: one-person, one-vote. In this, as in several other arenas, scholars thought the political question doctrine all but dead.[10]

The Precedents on Gerrymandering

Since *Shaw v. Reno* (1993), the Court has insisted that when *race* is a predominant factor in redistricting—even to remedy past racial discrimination—the standard of review must be strict scrutiny: The government must show a compelling interest in employing this classification and the remedy must be narrowly tailored to achieve this interest, a very high bar to meet. The Court has frequently struck down congressional maps that unconstitutionally grouped voters based on racial classifications, including North Carolina's first redistricting plan after the 2010 census.

However, for years leading up to *Rucho*, the Court had not determined how to recognize, or what to do about, an excessively *partisan* gerrymander. The Court first addressed gerrymandering for purely partisan purposes in *Davis v. Bandemer* (1986), when Indiana Democrats claimed the state's congressional districts diluted their votes, violating the Fourteenth Amendment. While declining to overturn Indiana's districting scheme, the Court held that cases of partisan gerrymandering

---

[9]*Baker v. Carr*, 369 U.S. 186, 269–270 (1962), Justice Frankfurter dissent, quoting from his majority opinion in *Colegrove v. Green*, 328 U.S. 549, 556 (1946).

[10]See Gwynne Skinner, "Misunderstood, Misconstrued, and Now Clearly Dead: The 'Political Question Doctrine' as a Justiciability Doctrine," 29 *Journal of Law and Politics* 427–599 (Spring 2014).

were justiciable—with important qualifications. "Unconstitutional discrimination occurs only when the electoral system is arranged in a manner that will consistently degrade a voter's or a group of voters' influence on the political process as a whole," and "plaintiffs were required to prove both intentional discrimination against an identifiable political group and an actual discriminatory effect on that group." The Court "clearly foreclose[d] any claim that the Constitution requires proportional representation, or that legislatures… must draw district lines to come as near as possible to allocating seats to the contending parties in proportion to what their anticipated statewide vote will be."[11]

In 2004, the Court again confronted the question of partisan gerrymandering in *Vieth v. Jubilerer*. Plaintiffs challenged Pennsylvania's congressional districts, redrawn following the 2000 census, as providing an unfair advantage to the state's Republican Party and violating (as in *Bandemer*) the Fourteenth Amendment. Justice Scalia's plurality opinion, supported by three other Justices, argued that the Court had been wrong in finding partisan gerrymandering justiciable in *Bandemer*. While Justice Kennedy concurred in the judgment, he refused to foreclose the possibility that the Court could be presented with a judicially manageable standard in the future, thwarting a majority decision to overturn *Bandemer*.

The Efficiency Gap, the First Amendment, and the Fourteenth Amendment

In the October 2017 term, the Court took up *Benisek v. Lamone* (the case that would return in the 2018 term) along with Wisconsin's partisan gerrymandering case, *Gill v. Whitford*.[12] The Wisconsin case attempted a mathematical solution to Justice Kennedy's *Vieth* quest for a manageable standard for identifying extreme partisan gerrymanders.

---

[11]*Davis v. Bandemer*, 478 U.S. 109, 111, 127, 130 (1986).
[12]See Chapter 3 of *SCOTUS 2018*, "*Gill v. Whitford* on Partisan Gerrymandering," by Alex Keena, Michael Latner, Anthony McGann, and Charles Smith.

The *Gill* plaintiffs advanced a formula for an election "efficiency gap," calculating what percentage of either party's vote had been "wasted" by voting for a losing candidate or providing unneeded votes to a winning candidate, arguing a gap of more than 7% would give one party an advantage substantial enough to trigger a constitutional violation (Wisconsin's was greater).[13]

In both cases, the Court sidestepped the core issue. In *Gill*, the Justices unanimously remanded the case to the lower court, insisting that to establish standing, plaintiffs needed to demonstrate that their *own* electoral district had been unfairly drawn instead of challenging the entire state map. In *Benisek*, the Court upheld the district court's denial of a preliminary injunction in the Maryland mapping case, allowing the maps to stand pending the *Gill* decision. The conservative Justices also made clear that the efficiency gap calculation was unlikely to solve the challenge of establishing a manageable standard; in the oral arguments, Chief Justice Roberts referred to the mathematical formulas as "sociological gobbledygook" that did not provide any meaningful guidance on identifying a constitutional violation.[14] However, Justice Kennedy hinted that an argument about First Amendment associational rights could replace the more-common equal protection argument.

The next term, the Court once again took up partisan gerrymandering in *Rucho* and *Lamone*. Justice Kennedy had retired, and his seat now belonged to Justice Brett Kavanaugh. In oral argument, Justice Kavanaugh conceded that partisan gerrymandering constituted a real problem but seemed inclined to leave the matter up to the states.[15] Justice Breyer was the only member of the Court to attempt to construct an explicit formula, suggesting in oral argument that the Court should get involved *only* if a party gained over two-thirds of the seats without winning a majority of the vote (as in North Carolina) *and* their

---

[13] *Gill v. Whitford* 585 U.S. ___ (2018). See Robin I. Mordfin, "Proving Partisan Gerrymandering with the Efficiency Gap," University of Chicago Law School, 25 September 2017.

[14] *Gill v. Whitford* oral argument transcript, page 40.

[15] *Rucho* oral argument transcript, page 68.

Congressional map has been drawn by the state legislature, not by an independent redistricting commission.[16]

The efficiency gap rationale and the search for a mathematical formula had been all but abandoned. In their *Rucho* brief, Common Cause litigants were careful to explain that they were instead seeking a *legal* standard; mathematical data were simply being used to support their argument.[17] They suggested the legal standard should employ a test based on the Court's own precedents and grounded in two possible constitutional foundations: the Fourteenth Amendment's guarantee of equal protection and the First Amendment's right to free association.

Under the equal protection argument, an unconstitutional partisan gerrymander would (1) have a district-level discriminatory *intent* against one political party; (2) have a statewide discriminatory *effect* against that political party that is likely to persist; and (3) lack a legitimate legislative explanation for the composition of districts.[18] By following the Court's apportionment and racial redistricting precedents, vote dilution would be considered unconstitutional when based on partisan identity, as it was when based on racial identity.[19]

The First Amendment argument hinged on a right to free association impeded by districts intentionally drawn to dilute the votes of one party. This argument emphasized the *consequences* of gerrymandered districts: One political party's diminished ability to organize, fundraise, and garner support. This effect would constitute discrimination on the basis of belief and association of the kind expressly prohibited by the First Amendment. A First Amendment test would hold a districting map unconstitutional if the Court found (1) proof of *intent* to burden individuals based on their partisan belief and affiliation; (2) an *actual* burden on political speech; and (3) a *causal link* between the two.[20] Proponents of this approach (including Justice Kagan) suggested

---

[16]Ibid., pages 11–12.

[17]Motion to Affirm by the *Common Cause* Appellees, page 31.

[18]*Rucho* oral argument transcript, page 48.

[19]Guy-Uriel E. Charles and Luis E. Fuentes-Rohwer, "Symposium: Precedent Dictates a Win for the Plaintiffs in this Term's Partisan-Gerrymandering Cases," SCOTUSblog, 7 February 2019.

[20]*Rucho* decision, page 25.

a balancing test employing a 1983 precedent finding burdens on the associational rights of independent voters and candidates, where the claim of a burdened right to association is strengthened when the harm disproportionately affects one party.[21] The precedent for an associational balancing test is extensive and has been used as recently as 2008.[22] The First Amendment rationale in the gerrymandering context was new to the Court in the *Rucho* and *Lamone* arguments, a likely result of Kennedy's expressed interest in *Gill*.

The respondents argued that the plurality had been right in *Vieth*: The Court should overturn *Bandemer* and shift partisan gerrymandering claims away from the federal courts. "This Court has repeatedly failed to identify a justiciable standard for partisan gerrymandering claims" not because of "a lack of judicial imagination or a lack of claims that the particular map before the Court was the most extreme ever" but because of "the basic decision of the framers to give responsibility for congressional districting to political actors."[23] From this perspective, redistricting belonged to the state legislatures; federal courts had no business intervening. Even if the Court rejected the claim that districting belonged to the legislature, plaintiffs had still failed to establish a judicially manageable standard. Any attempt to curb partisan gerrymandering ran the risk of tying the hands of the legislature with an arbitrary standard.

A "Political Question"

In the end, both the First and Fourteenth Amendment arguments against partisan gerrymandering failed. The 5-4 decision in *Rucho*, split along ideological lines, ultimately refused to accept any standard by which to declare these—and, indeed, any instances—of partisan

---

[21] *Anderson v. Celebrezze* 460 U.S. 780 (1983).

[22] *Crawford v. Marion County Election Board* 553 U.S. 181 (2008); Daniel Tojaki, "Symposium: How to Win the Partisan-Gerrymandering Cases," SCOTUSblog, 6 February 2019.

[23] *Rucho* oral argument transcript, page 3.

redistricting unconstitutional; it was a non-justiciable political question. Writing for the Court, Chief Justice Roberts noted the history of gerrymandering as a practice; statements made by Madison and Hamilton during the Constitutional convention showed that the Framers understood the potential for partisan gerrymandering when vesting districting power in the legislative branch, and they considered this risk a necessary evil for a functioning representative democracy. His opinion held that Article I's time, place, and manner clause established no limits for what the legislature could take into account in drawing congressional districts.[24]

Roberts differentiated partisan gerrymandering from apportionment, which the Court had deemed justiciable in *Baker v. Carr*. An apportionment "claim could be decided under basic equal protection principles"—it was simple enough to determine when votes were diluted by districts with unequal populations. But Roberts dismissed each of the standards offered to identify excessively partisan gerrymanders. Rejecting the Fourteenth Amendment vote dilution test, he noted the difficulty in determining both intent and effect; federal judges should not be asked to predict the future and speculate about lasting effects of misdrawn districts. The First Amendment test was too broad: It would bar *all* partisan considerations in the design of districts, without a mechanism for determining when gerrymandering went too far.[25] Too much subjective judicial decision-making would still be required.

Justice Kagan's impassioned dissent was joined by Justices Ginsburg, Breyer, and Sotomayor. She took the unusual step of reading large portions of the dissent from the bench. She argued that the tests proposed for identifying egregious gerrymanders *were* adequate to resolve the issue of justiciability; she and Justice Sotomayor had observed, in oral argument, the extremity of the North Carolina districts (of 24,000 possible maps generated by a computer, the map selected had a greater partisan skew than 99% of them) as evidence that standards existed to

---

[24]*Rucho* decision, pages 10, 30.

[25]Ibid., pages 11, 23, 26.

identify outliers.[26] The dissenters noted that lower courts had nearly unanimously agreed on when to strike down legislative maps.[27]

Justice Kagan also made a broader argument about the tremendous damage done to democracy and democratic values by the rise in partisan gerrymandering, noting that the use of technology increased the efficacy of partisan gerrymandering to a degree unimaginable by the Founders. Kagan emphasized (and, indeed, the conservative majority seemed to concede) that partisan gerrymandering was incompatible with the democratic principles of fair elections and equal access to the ballot box. The majority's decision to abandon any effort to identify even the most extreme partisan gerrymanders prevents the Court from protecting access to the political process. The majority decision upheld conditions in which "politicians' incentives conflict with voters' interests, leaving citizens without any political remedy for their constitutional harms."[28] She concluded:

> The practices challenged in these cases imperil our system of government. Part of the Court's role in that system is to defend its foundations. None is more important than free and fair elections. With respect but deep sadness, I dissent.[29]

What Remains?

Rucho settled the matter as far as the federal courts are concerned. Political gerrymandering's harm to the political process cannot, at present, be expressed as a constitutional grievance. The Supreme Court, criticized by some for more than fifty years of imprudent involvement in political conflicts, appeared to breathe new life into the political questions doctrine.

---

[26]*Rucho* oral argument transcript, pages 28–29.

[27]*Rucho* Kagan dissent, page 15.

[28]Ibid., pages 9, 8, and 29, quoting her concurrence in *Gill*.

[29]Ibid., page 33.

What recourse remains? During oral argument, Justice Gorsuch referenced the use of state ballot initiatives (employed in Colorado and Michigan) to curb partisan gerrymandering. Justice Kavanaugh underscored an increase in state activity regulating gerrymandering as evidence that there remain options outside of the Supreme Court to solve the problem. Litigants noted a bill regularly passed in the House (in 2019, HR-1) mandating independent redistricting commissions, as another method of solving the problem.[30] While state legislatures generally draw electoral maps, eight states have authorized independent commissions to draw districts under the presumption that such a commission will be less partisan, a practice narrowly upheld in *Arizona State Legislature v. Arizona Redistricting Commission* (2015).[31] Finally, Gorsuch emphasized that the Court's decision would in no way preclude *state* courts from ruling against gerrymandering under state constitutions.[32]

However, despite these proffered solutions, the Supreme Court's decision in *Rucho* changed the landscape of partisan gerrymandering. With federal courts removed from the partisan redistricting issue, state legislatures have nearly carte blanche to construct districts in as skewed a manor as they choose following the 2020 census.

---

[30]Rucho oral argument transcript, pages 16, 17 and 70. The Senate, as of this writing, has no intention of voting on the bill.

[31]The dissent by Chief Justice Roberts, in which Justices Scalia, Alito, and Thomas joined, held that Article I §4 clearly assigned redistricting to state legislatures, yet this remedy was one mentioned by the *Rucho* majority.

[32]In 2017, the Pennsylvania Supreme Court struck down the state's congressional map as an unlawful political gerrymander.

12

Timbs v. Indiana on Excessive Fines and Civil Forfeitures

Marian R. Williams

The Eighth Amendment to the US Constitution states that, "Excessive bail shall not be required, nor excessive fines imposed, nor cruel and unusual punishments inflicted." The Supreme Court has never said whether this clause of the Constitution protects people against excessive fines levied by *state* or *local* governments. In *Timbs v. Indiana*, the Court finally addressed the issue in a case dealing with civil asset forfeiture. The Court put to rest lingering questions about not only incorporation of the Excessive Fines Clause, but also whether or not the clause applies to civil asset forfeiture, an increasingly common feature of American law enforcement.

M. R. Williams (✉)
Department of Government and Justice Studies,
Appalachian State University, Boone, NC, USA
e-mail: williamsmr4@appstate.edu

© The Author(s) 2020
D. Klein and M. Marietta (eds.), *SCOTUS 2019*,
https://doi.org/10.1007/978-3-030-29956-9_12

123

Incorporation of the Excessive Fines Clause

No doubt most Americans assume that the enumeration of rights in the first ten amendments to the Constitution protects them against the actions of their state and local governments. This is largely true today. However, it was not true for much of US history, and even today it is not entirely true. Nearly 190 years ago, in a decision that has never been overruled, the Supreme Court held that the Bill of Rights, having been designed to allay fears that the newly created national government would abuse its powers, imposed limitations *only* on the national government.[1] (Note that the very first words of the Bill of Rights are "*Congress* shall make no law…" but the Amendments do not mention state governments.) Some states included similar protections within their own state constitutions, but not all did; thus, for many years the rights of individuals were not as protected from state encroachments as they were from federal encroachments.

When the Fourteenth Amendment was passed in the wake of the Civil War, it contained important protections of individuals against state governments, most notably in the Privileges and Immunities, Equal Protection, and Due Process Clauses. In a lengthy and fitful process that began near the end of the nineteenth century and is often referred to as "selective incorporation," the Supreme Court has held that most of the rights listed in the Bill of Rights apply against state governments through the Fourteenth Amendment. Prior to the Court's ruling in *Timbs*, the most recently incorporated right was the Second Amendment's right to bear arms, in 2010.[2] After *Timbs*, only a few rights remain unincorporated. Curiously, and controversially, incorporation has happened through the Due Process Clause, which commands states not to deprive individuals of "life, liberty, and property without due process of law," rather than the more natural looking Privileges and Immunities Clause ("No state shall make or enforce any law which shall abridge the privileges or immunities of citizens of the United States").

---

[1] *Barron v. Baltimore*, 32 U.S. 243 (1833).
[2] *McDonald v. Chicago*, 561 U. S. 742 (2010).

Why Is Asset Forfeiture Important?

Although the Supreme Court focused primarily on the incorporation of the Excessive Fines Clause, the significance of the *Timbs* ruling regarding the practice of civil asset forfeiture cannot be ignored. Asset forfeiture is the process by which a local, state, or federal government agency seizes property from an individual who is suspected of criminal activity. This action can be against the individual's assets that were used in the commission of a crime (known as *in personam* forfeiture), or it can also be conducted against the property itself (known as an *in rem* forfeiture). It may sound odd for the state to act against property when the owner is the one losing it. But sometimes it is clear that property—like a boat or car—was used in crimes like the drug trade while it is not clear which individual was involved. The boat may have been "guilty" of carrying drugs even if the owner was never charged or convicted. And since only individuals (and not property), have rights, *in rem* forfeitures can occur without an arrest, let alone conviction, of an individual. *In rem* forfeiture is more commonly referred to as civil asset forfeiture to distinguish it from forfeitures associated with a criminal prosecution against an individual.

Civil asset forfeiture is a lucrative business for federal and state governments; between 2001 and 2014, the US Department of Justice and the US Department of the Treasury collected nearly $29 billion from these actions.[3] The proceeds collected through state civil asset forfeitures are largely unknown, however, because of the lack of reporting by local law enforcement. One study found that 14 states collected $250 million from civil asset forfeitures in 2013 alone.[4] Other research has shown that local and state police agencies employ the proceeds of civil asset

---

[3]See Dick Carpenter, Lisa Knepper, and Jennifer McDonald, *Policing for Profit: The Abuse of Civil Asset Forfeiture*, 2nd Edition.

[4]See Jefferson E. Holcomb, Marian R. Williams, William D. Hicks, Tomislav V. Kovandzic, and Michele Bisaccia Meitl, "Civil Asset Forfeiture Laws and Equitable Sharing Activity by the Police," 17 *Criminology & Public Policy* 101 (2018).

forfeitures to offset budget shortfalls, to purchase additional equipment, or to hire more officers, a practice criticized as "policing for profit."[5] Since data on state civil asset forfeitures are limited, it is possible that states are collecting more proceeds from these forfeitures than the federal government.

Although the *Bajakajian* ruling attempted to develop standards for determining the excessiveness of fines, one of its standards ignores a common practice: *civil asset forfeiture in the absence of a criminal conviction*.[6] Only eighteen states require a criminal conviction before forfeiture can occur; thus, *in rem* forfeitures occur more frequently in the states. The second standard in *Bajakajian*—taking into account the maximum punishment that could have been imposed under the sentencing guidelines for the offense—is not applicable to *in rem* proceedings if no criminal conviction occurs. This means that lower courts may have difficulty assessing excessiveness when there are no charges, no conviction, and no punishment upon which to base the decision. As a result, lower courts will continue to provide inconsistent rulings about what is considered excessive with regard to civil asset forfeiture.

Although *Timbs* dealt with *in rem* forfeiture, the main thrust of the decision is the application of the Excessive Fines Clause to the states. Aside from the effect it could have on *in rem* forfeitures, some hope that the ruling will apply to "poverty penalties" in criminal cases. Beyond criminal fines, this would include court costs, restitution, and other administrative fees that are imposed on offenders who are convicted of a crime. While many offenders are unable to pay even the smallest amount of fines and fees, the inability to pay could result in the suspension of licenses, loss of public benefits, or additional fees for defaulting. As a result, some offenders go without food, housing, and medicine in order to pay their fines.[7] In other instances, offenders who cannot pay may be placed on probation instead; however, even these individuals

---

[5]Carpenter, Knepper, and McDonald, *Policing for Profit*. See also Kathleen Baicker and Mirielle Jacobsen, "Finders Keepers: Forfeiture Laws, Policing Incentives, and Local Budgets".
[6]*U.S. v. Bajakajian*, 524 U.S. 321 (1998).
[7]See Beth Colgan, "The Excessive Fines Clause: Challenging the Modern Debtor's Prison," 65 *UCLA Law Review* 2 (2018).

are required to pay some form of fine or fees. For individuals placed on probation outright, as opposed to those who are placed on probation because they cannot pay their fines, many have fines and fees imposed on them in addition to probation. As a result, many probationers find it difficult to fulfill their monetary obligations associated with their punishments. In *Bearden v. Georgia*, the Supreme Court ruled that it was "fundamentally unfair" for the state to revoke probation and then incarcerate offenders who cannot pay their fines.[8] Despite *Bearden*, a number of offenders are still jailed for their failure to pay their fines, leading for calls to rethink the use of fines, court costs, and other fees, especially for indigent offenders.[9] The focus on the offense for determining the amount of a fine (and whether it is excessive) could be replaced with an assessment of an offender's ability to pay. This type of policy would expand the excessive fines protections afforded in *Bajakajian* and the due process protections afforded in *Bearden*.

Background of the Case

In 2013, Tyson Timbs pleaded guilty to dealing in a controlled substance and conspiracy to commit theft. He was sentenced to one year of house arrest, five years of probation, and was assessed a $10,000 fine. In addition, the state of Indiana initiated a civil forfeiture proceeding against Timbs' Land Rover valued at $42,000, because of the likelihood that the vehicle was used to transport heroin. The trial court denied this request, stating that the forfeiture of the vehicle was "grossly disproportionate" to the level of Timbs' crime, as the value of the vehicle was over four times as much as the fine assessed against Timbs. The Indiana Court of Appeals agreed with the trial court that this violated the Eighth Amendment's Excessive Fines Clause. The Indiana Supreme Court, however, did not address the issue of proportionality with regard

---

[8]461 U.S. 660 (1983) at 661.

[9]See Shaila Dewan, "Court Conundrum: Offenders Who Can't Pay, or Won't," *The New York Times*, 26 September 2015.

to the forfeiture. Instead, the court simply stated that the Excessive Fines Clause does not apply to state action, since it had not been incorporated to the states, and ruled in the state's favor. Timbs appealed to the US Supreme Court.

Issues Involved in the Case

Although some have framed the *Timbs* case as a repudiation of civil asset forfeiture, the case is really an argument about Excessive Fines.[10] The *Timbs* case simply involved a test of that right under state law using civil asset forfeiture. The Court's opinion, penned by Justice Ginsburg, is an examination of the history and importance of the Excessive Fines Clause and only a small portion points to the civil asset forfeiture involved in the case. The first portion of Justice Ginsburg's opinion highlights that the Fourteenth Amendment's Due Process Clause has enabled most of the Bill of Rights to be incorporated—those rights that are considered "fundamental" and "deeply rooted."[11] The second portion of Justice Ginsburg's opinion illustrates why the Excessive Fines Clause exhibits these traits. Beginning with Magna Carta in 1215 and continuing with the English Bill of Rights in 1689, the right against Excessive Fines was enshrined in English law and continued with colonial-era prohibitions. When the Fourteenth Amendment was ratified in 1868, 35 out of the existing 37 states prohibited excessive fines; however, Black Codes and similar laws imposed fines on individuals for minor infractions such as vagrancy and imposed involuntary labor if fines could not be paid. Today, all 50 states prohibit excessive fines in some manner.

In the third and final portion of Justice Ginsburg's opinion, the applicability of the Excessive Fines Clause to *in rem* proceedings is addressed. In particular, the state of Indiana argues that, even if the Excessive Fines Clause is incorporated to the states, it does not apply

---

[10]See Scott Bullock and Nick Sibilla, "The Supreme Court Resuscitates the Eighth Amendment: The Justices Strike a Blow Against Policing for Profit," *The Atlantic*, 13 March 2019.

[11]See *McDonald v. City of Chicago*, 561 U.S. 742 (2010).

to *in rem* forfeitures because this is not considered "fundamental" or "deeply rooted." Justice Ginsburg points to the Court's unanimous ruling in *Austin v United States*,[12] in which the Court ruled that the Excessive Fines Clause applies to civil penalties that are at least partially punitive. As a result, the *Timbs* case produced two rulings. First, the Excessive Fines Clause must be incorporated to the states. Second, *in rem* proceedings that result in punitive outcomes fall under the protection of the Excessive Fines Clause.

Justice Gorsuch and Justice Thomas provided concurring opinions in this case, examining the issue through the lens of the Privileges and Immunities Clause of the Fourteenth Amendment, which states that, "[n]o State shall make or enforce any law which shall abridge the privileges and immunities of citizens of the United States." Justice Thomas states that the Due Process Clause only deals with "process," but not substantive rights. Instead, Thomas argues that the terms "privileges" and "immunities" were synonymous with "rights" when the Fourteenth Amendment was ratified and that "the ratifying public understood the Privileges and Immunities Clause to protect constitutionally enumerated rights against interference by the states."[13] Accordingly, the protection against excessive fines was incorporated against the states as one of the inalienable rights granted by the Bill of Rights.

Constitutional Significance

Both Justice Ginsburg and Justice Thomas provide a detailed account of the significance of the Excessive Fines Clause going back to Magna Carta in 1215. That the prohibition against excessive fines has existed for hundreds of years raises the question of why it was one of the last rights incorporated to the states. The brief for the state of Indiana provides a glimpse into this issue. According to the state of Indiana, historically, the prohibition against excessive fines was invoked for *in personam*

---

[12]509 U.S. 602 (1993).
[13]*Timbs* Thomas concurrence, page 3.

proceedings and colonial (and then state) governments did not enforce the prohibition for *in rem* proceedings. The state of Indiana argued that the punishment aspect of criminal asset forfeiture against an *individual* was distinct from a civil forfeiture against *property*; thus, the Excessive Fines Clause should not apply to *in rem* proceedings.[14] However, this argument is inconsistent with the US Supreme Court ruling in *Austin v. United States*, where the Court ruled that partially punitive civil forfeitures are protected by the Excessive Fines Clause.[15] The key issue was that *Austin* involved civil asset forfeiture by the federal government, so this ruling does not hold in the states unless the Excessive Fines Clause is incorporated to the states, which is the question in *Timbs*.

In addition, the Court in *Austin* declined to provide an interpretation of what is "excessive" under the Clause, leaving the lower courts to decide the matter. Later, the Court tried to provide guidance to lower courts about what is "excessive" in *United States v. Bajakajian*. In this case, the defendant failed to report over $350,000 to customs officials as he and his family were leaving the country, a violation of federal law. Bajakajian pleaded guilty and, while the government wanted to forfeit the entire amount of money, the District Court stated that, based on the offense, the forfeiture of the entire amount was "grossly disproportional to the offense in question" and reduced the amount of the forfeiture to $15,000, in addition to three years' probation and a $5000 fine.[16] The issue in this case was not the forfeiture of $15,000 (which Bajakajian did not challenge as excessive), but the attempted forfeiture of the total $357,144 that Bajakajian did not report. In *Bajakajian*, the US Supreme Court noted three standards to determine if a forfeiture is "grossly disproportional." The first is whether the offender fits the "class of persons for whom the statute was principally designed; in this case, money launderers, drug traffickers, and tax evaders," which Bajakajian was not.[17] The second takes into account the maximum punishment

---

[14]See Kris Fernandez, "*Timbs v. Indiana*: The Constitutionality of Civil Forfeiture When Used by the States," 14 *Duke Journal of Constitutional Law & Public Policy* 1 (2019).

[15]509 U.S. 602 (1993) at 602–603.

[16]524 U.S. 321 (1998) at 321.

[17]Ibid., at 338.

that could have been imposed under the sentencing guidelines for the offense; in this case, a 6-month sentence and a $5000 fine. The third examines the harm caused by the defendant; in this case, the harm that Bajakajian caused was minimal, according to the Court. Based on these indices, the Court affirmed that the forfeiture of the $357,144 was grossly disproportional.

If the Court felt that the standards for determining excessiveness in *Bajakajian* were clear, in practice, they have proved to be problematic. Lower courts have been inconsistent in applying these standards, with only four forfeitures found to be excessive in the first fifteen years after *Bajakajian* was decided.[18] Additionally, even though the Court articulated in both *Austin* and *Bajakajian* that the Excessive Fines Clause can apply to *in rem* forfeitures, these cases feature forfeitures conducted by the federal government, not state governments. This illustrates the importance of *Timbs v. Indiana*—applying the Excessive Fines Clause to *in rem* forfeitures by state governments, which engage in these types of forfeitures much more often than the federal government. A problem, however, that none of these cases decided, including *Timbs*, is what is considered "excessive," leaving it up to lower courts to decide.

Conclusion

Applying the right against excessive fines to the states marks another step toward total incorporation of the Bill of Rights. It remains to be seen how *Timbs* will affect the practice of civil asset forfeiture at the state and local level. There are other common practices as well to which the Excessive Fines Clause may apply, including the use of fines, fees, and court costs in the criminal justice system. While *Timbs* is seen by some as a blow to civil asset forfeiture, it does not stop its practice and lower courts will be given the discretion of deciding what is "excessive" when such forfeitures take place.

---

[18]See David Pimentel, "Forfeitures and the Eighth Amendment: A Practical Approach to the Excessive Fines Clause as a Check on Government Seizures," 11 *Harvard Law & Policy Review* 541 (2017).

13

Other Major Cases

David Klein

The Supreme Court handed down far more notable decisions this past
term than a book this size can cover. This chapter provides brief over-
views of several additional decisions that we think worthy of readers'
attention both for insights they offer into the Justices' thinking and
for their potential to affect the development of legal doctrines and
how those doctrines influence everyday life. We begin with three that
were each decided 5-4, with the Republican appointees (Chief Justice
Roberts, and Justices Thomas, Alito, Gorsuch, and Kavanaugh) in
the majority and the four Democratic appointees (Justices Ginsburg,
Breyer, Sotomayor, and Kagan) dissenting.

Lamps Plus, Inc. v. Varela extended a 2010 decision of the Court.[1]
Together the decisions establish that one party to a dispute cannot force
the other party to submit to class-wide arbitration unless the contract

---

[1] *Stolt-Nielsen S. A. v. Animal Feeds Int'l Corp.*, 559 U.S. 662 (2010).

D. Klein (✉)
Eastern Michigan University, Ypsilanti, MI, USA
e-mail: dklein2@emich.edu

© The Author(s) 2020
D. Klein and M. Marietta (eds.), *SCOTUS 2019*,
https://doi.org/10.1007/978-3-030-29956-9_13

between the two parties unambiguously permits it. That might sound dry and technical, but it has important implications for one of sharpest ongoing battles in the legal world—between people (mostly liberal) who feel that individuals involved in disputes with wealthy and powerful entities do not have adequate access to courts and people (mostly conservative) who seek to limit access to courts because of worries about irresponsible plaintiffs, plaintiffs' attorneys, and juries.

Arbitration, being less formal and legalistic than court proceedings, can produce quicker and less expensive resolutions to disputes. For this reason, it has long been common for companies negotiating a contract to include a clause requiring that any dispute between them be resolved in arbitration, rather than court. Recognizing the value of arbitration, in 1925 Congress passed the Federal Arbitration Act directing courts to respect these clauses.

In recent years, arbitration clauses have mushroomed far beyond companies' suppliers, to their contracts with consumers and employees. Arbitration continues to be attractive to companies for its efficiency, privacy, absence of juries, and limited connection to the law. (Arbitration decisions are rarely reviewable by courts and don't contribute to legal precedent.)

There is one type of suit large companies are especially eager to avoid—class-action lawsuits. In a class action, many plaintiffs with fairly small claims band together to file a single lawsuit. *Lamps Plus* itself provides an example of where a class action would be attractive. A company employee was tricked by a hacker into disclosing the tax information of approximately 1300 other employees. This of course caused serious inconvenience and anxiety for many employees—Varela had to deal with a fraudulent federal tax return filed in his name—and it is understandable that they wanted to be compensated by their employer. Still, the amount of compensation they could hope to receive was fairly small, and the cost of individual proceedings (whether in court or arbitration) would likely exceed that amount. In such situations, which are common, potential plaintiffs have only two rational options: either forgo compensation or band together to share the costs of a single proceeding. If allowed to combine, not only can they use their resources more efficiently, but their negotiating position becomes much stronger, as the defendant stands to lose a large amount of money in the single proceeding. Defendants do not always oppose class actions—sometimes defending a single case can be more efficient for them too—but they worry about abuse of the procedure by attorneys who can hope to earn massive legal fees by aggregating numerous small claims into a single very large one.

When Varela attempted to file a class-action *lawsuit* in this case, he was turned away by the court because he had signed an arbitration clause. This was a routine occurrence, not at all remarkable. The interesting part is what came next. Varela insisted that he should be allowed to bring his arbitration claim as a class action on behalf of all the affected employees. The trial and appellate courts agreed with him, but the Supreme Court reversed.

To the Supreme Court majority, the key premise was that arbitration requires consent. Because the company had not clearly consented to class-action arbitration in the contract, only individual arbitration would be allowed. The dissenters agreed with the premise but argued that it should point courts in the opposite direction. It is well known that the characteristics that make arbitration attractive to large companies make it less attractive to many consumers and employees. But then why would they sign contracts including arbitration clauses? The answer, said the dissenters, is because they have no choice—if they refuse, they just don't get the job or the product. Viewed this way, there's no genuine consent to use arbitration in the first place.

Whatever the merits of this argument, it was unsuccessful. The result, when combined with a number of other recent decisions on class actions and arbitrations, is that individual arbitration is the one path open to a great many employees and consumers in most situations where disputes arise.

In *Franchise Tax Board of California v. Hyatt*, the Court overruled a forty-year-old precedent[2] and held that the courts of one state cannot hear lawsuits brought by a private citizen against another state. In so doing, it built on several more recent decisions that expanded

---

[2] *Nevada* v. *Hall*, 440 U.S. 410 (1979).

states' immunity to lawsuits, with the result that there are now very few situations in which a private citizen can sue any state in any court without the state's consent.[3] Because each of these earlier rulings was made by a bare majority voting along ideological lines, few close observers of the Supreme Court could have been very surprised by either the outcome of *Hyatt* or the voting lineup.

The opinions in *Hyatt* devote considerable space to the question of whether, between the time of the Declaration of Independence and the ratification of the Constitution, the states' immunity from suit in each other's courts was absolute or only a matter of courtesy between states. But the real issue dividing the Justices goes much deeper. When the colonies declared their independence from Great Britain, they became autonomous actors, not answering to each other or a higher authority. With the ratification of the Constitution in 1788, the new states gave up some, but not all, of that autonomy. Almost all Americans (including the Justices) will agree with those basic propositions. But Americans have never been able to agree about exactly how much autonomy the states should retain.

The *Hyatt* case helps illustrate what is at stake in this question. After Hyatt had moved from California to Nevada to reduce his taxes, he was aggressively investigated by a California tax agency that suspected he had underpaid his California taxes. (According to the Supreme Court of Nevada, the agency "sent over 100 letters and demands for information to third parties," and many of these "contained Hyatt's social security number or home address or both.")[4] Suppose that Hyatt was allowed to bring his case and won. That outcome would likely dissuade this agency—and other agencies—from acting as aggressively in the future. One result would be to make individuals somewhat safer from oppressive behavior by state governments. However, this would come with a cost: less active and forceful pursuit of state interests.

---

[3]*Seminole Tribe of Florida v. Florida*, 517 U.S. 44 (1996); *Alden v. Maine*, 527 U.S. 706 (1999); *Board of Trustees of Univ. of Ala. v. Garrett*, 531 U.S. 356 (2001); *Coleman v. Court of Appeals of Md.*, 566 U.S. 30 (2012).

[4]*Franchise Tax Bd. of Cal. v. Hyatt*, 407 P.3d 717 (Nev. 2017).

Contemporary conservatives generally view state governments as more responsive and innovative than the federal government and as a crucial counterweight to its power. Liberals are typically less trustful of state governments. It is important to avoid caricatures; few liberals deny the value of healthy state governments, and few conservatives think state governments should have free rein to do whatever they want. But liberals tend to give somewhat greater emphasis to the protection of individuals, while conservatives give somewhat greater emphasis to maintaining state autonomy. Because the Constitution's only explicit exemption from lawsuit is the Eleventh Amendment's rule that a state cannot be sued *in federal court* by a citizen of another state or country, the extension of immunity to other situations has rested on arguments about the structure of the Constitution and principles underlying it. Liberal Justices have fiercely contested these arguments, but they have been unable to win the votes of any conservative Justices. The result, as reflected in the *Hyatt* decision, is the increasingly firm entrenchment of a concept of "sovereign immunity" under which states enjoy extensive protection from private lawsuits.

Knick v. Township of Scott involved another attempt to contest the exercise of state power in court. Here, the power in question was eminent domain, by which a government can take private property without the owner's consent. The only constitutional restrictions on this power (found in the Fifth Amendment) are that the taking be for a "public use" and that the owner receive "just compensation" for the property.

In this case, Knick felt that a township ordinance requiring her to open a gravesite on her land to the public during daylight hours amounted to a taking of property. She sued in federal court to either block the ordinance or be compensated for the intrusion. The federal court dismissed her case, saying that she first had to seek compensation through state legal proceedings. In doing so, the court followed a 1985 Supreme Court decision, where the Court held that "a property owner has not suffered a violation of the Just Compensation Clause until the owner has unsuccessfully attempted to obtain just compensation through the procedures provided by the State for obtaining such compensation."[5] The Court in *Knick* overruled this precedent, holding that the constitutional "violation is complete at the time of the taking" and, therefore, "pursuit of a remedy in federal court need not await any subsequent state action."[6]

It is not obvious that aggrieved property owners should expect to win cases more often or more speedily in federal court than they would in state court. But whatever its practical effects turn out to be, the ruling and overruling in *Knick* affirm the importance of property rights. Because most contemporary advocates of greater protection for property rights are conservatives, the *Knick* decision, even though it differs from the other two decisions in favoring plaintiffs, is as much a victory for conservatives as they are.

The next case, **Nieves v. Bartlett**, combines another ideologically loaded issue—defendant's rights—with the right to free speech, which does not divide liberals and conservatives so neatly. Imagine that you participate in a rally criticizing your local police force. Even if police officers who are present to keep the peace are offended by what you say, they can't arrest you simply for saying it. To do so would violate your First Amendment right to free speech.

But there are lots of other things they can arrest you for—in many places even minor offenses like jaywalking or littering. What if you drop a gum wrapper on the ground, a police officer arrests you for littering, and you believe the officer's *real* reason for arresting you was that he didn't like the opinion you were expressing at the rally. Can you sue the police officer for violating your rights and realistically hope to win the lawsuit? If not, how can we make sure the right to free speech is adequately protected? If so, how can we make sure that police officers' fear of being sued doesn't interfere with their ability to make the difficult and unpopular decisions we need them to make to maintain public safety and order?

---

[5]*Williamson County Regional Planning Comm'n* v. *Hamilton Bank of Johnson City*, 473 U.S. 172 (1985).

[6]*Knick* decision, page 20.

It was these weighty underlying issues that drove the thinking of the Justices in this case, which revolved around interference with police efforts to prevent underage drinking at the "Arctic Man" festival in Alaska. The Court came down strongly on the side of police officers, ruling that they should almost always win if there was "probable cause" to arrest. However, the Court did allow for one potentially important exception: even if there was probable cause, a plaintiff can still win by presenting "objective evidence" that the police didn't arrest "otherwise similarly situated individuals not engaged in the same sort of protected speech."[7]

Three Justices argued that this approach is insufficiently protective of individuals. Two of these—Ginsburg and Sotomayor—will not come as a surprise, but the third—Gorsuch—might. Although consistently conservative in other areas of law, Gorsuch has shown considerable willingness to vote in favor of defendants, with or without the company of the other conservatives. For instance, he cast pro-defendant votes in several of the cases covered in this volume, perhaps most notably *U.S. v. Davis* (see below), *Haymond,* and *Gamble*—in which he and Justice Ginsburg were the only dissenters. (On the other hand, he was one of only two Justices to vote against the defendant in *Flowers.*) There is no space here to speculate about the reasons for his votes, but readers interested in criminal law may want to pay special attention to Gorsuch's votes and opinions.

Iancu v. Brunetti involved a very different issue of free speech. The federal statute governing trademark registration directs the US Patent and Trademark Office (PTO) to refuse registration to a trademark that "[c]onsists of or comprises immoral, deceptive, or scandalous matter."[8] When Eric Brunetti tried to register the trademark "FUCT" for his line of clothing, the PTO relied on that language to turn him down. Brunetti argued that this statutory language violates the First Amendment. When his case reached the Supreme Court, six Justices

---

[7] *Nieves* decision, page 14.
[8] 15 U.S.C. § 1052(a)

(Kagan, Thomas, Ginsburg, Alito, Gorsuch, and Kavanaugh) agreed with him.

The other three Justices (Roberts, Breyer, and Sotomayor) only partly disagreed. They felt that the term "scandalous" could be saved by reading it narrowly to bar only trademarks that are obscene or vulgar. But all nine Justices agreed that the word "immoral" didn't pass constitutional muster and had to go. More importantly, all nine agreed that it is unconstitutional for the government to refuse registration to a trademark because of the message it conveys. In doing so, they built on a 2017 decision that unanimously struck down the same statute's bar on trademarks that "disparage" other people.[9]

To understand the full import of this principle, consider PTO decisions to register the trademark D.A.R.E. TO RESIST DRUGS AND VIOLENCE but reject YOU CAN'T SPELL HEALTHCARE WITHOUT THC or to register WAR ON TERROR MEMORIAL but reject BABY AL QAEDA. The Court in *Brunetti* offers these as illustrations of decisions that are "understandable"—because the "rejected marks express opinions that are, at the least, offensive to many Americans"—but that nevertheless violate the First Amendment, because they "discriminate based on viewpoint."[10]

In enunciating this principle, the Justices were less concerned with protecting a specific instance of speech (they are as likely to be repulsed by a BABY AL QAEDA tee shirt as most other Americans) than with protecting speech in general. As Justice Alito wrote in his concurring opinion, "Our decision is not based on moral relativism but on the recognition that a law banning speech deemed by government officials to be 'immoral' or 'scandalous' can easily be exploited for illegitimate ends."[11]

The decision does not mean that the Constitution compels the government to permit trademarks like Brunetti's. None of the Justices ruled out the possibility that a more narrowly written statute focusing on the

---

[9]*Matal* v. *Tam*, 582 U.S. ___ (2017).
[10]*Brunetti* decision, page 8.
[11]*Brunetti* Alito concurrence, page 1.

mode, rather than substance, of the expression, could pass constitutional muster. Under a properly written statute, the PTO might be able to deny trademarks to a name like FUCT that, after all, conveys very little, if anything, in the way of a message.

Although arising in a very different context, the case of *U.S. v. Davis* also turned on the question whether a statute could reasonably be interpreted in a way that preserved its constitutionality. As in *Brunetti*, the Court's answer was no, though this time there were four dissenters and the disagreements between the Justices were more forceful.

Under the statute at issue in *Davis*, someone who "uses or carries a firearm" while committing a federal "crime of violence" is subject to a significantly longer prison sentence than if he committed the same crime without a firearm.[12] Davis and a partner were accused of several armed robberies in which they threatened store employees with sawed-off shotguns.[13] The jury found them guilty of the robberies, of the separate crime of conspiracy to commit robbery, and of using firearms in connection with both the robberies and the conspiracy. At sentencing, the judge imposed extra prison time on each defendant for both firearm counts.

Because the robberies readily fit the statute's definition of "crime of violence," the judge's decision to impose additional time for using a gun during them is easily justified and was not contested at the Supreme Court. What the Court had to grapple with was the additional prison time for using a gun in connection with the crime of conspiracy. The parties agreed that conspiracy did not satisfy the first part of the statute's two-part definition of "crime of violence," so everything hinged on the second prong of the definition: Whether the crime, "by its nature, involves a substantial risk that physical force against the person or property of another may be used in the course of committing the offense." The problem, said the Court, is that this definition is too vague to be constitutional. In doing so, it followed two recent precedents

---

[12]18 U.S.C. § 924(c).

[13]The reason these robberies were prosecutable as federal crimes is that they affected interstate commerce.

invalidating statutory provisions with nearly identical language. Justice Gorsuch wrote the Court's opinion and was joined by Justices Ginsburg, Breyer, Sotomayor, and Kagan.

American courts have long recognized that fundamental fairness requires crimes to be defined specifically enough for people to know how to avoid committing them and for the government to be able to enforce them in a non-arbitrary way. Imagine a legislature passed a law making it a crime to "use another person's private information without permission." So many actions might—or might not—violate this law that conscientious citizens would feel great anxiety, and almost surely some people would be prosecuted for certain actions while other people were not.

The four dissenters did not take issue with the premise that overly vague laws are unconstitutional; rather, they argued that this law, properly understood, was not particularly vague. Specifically, they contended that the second part of the definition should be read as inquiring into the defendant's conduct during the crime. The majority, focusing on the phrase "by its nature," rejected this reading as forced.

In contrast to several other cases described in this book, here we have an instance where the practical impact of a decision is much greater than its doctrinal impact. *Davis* probably will have little, if any, effect on how other judges analyze vagueness issues. But because it invalidated a provision that is relied on very frequently in federal prosecutions, it will raise questions about thousands of sentences already imposed and change the path of thousands of cases to come.

The antitrust case of ***Apple v. Pepper*** is similar in its potential for practical impact, though it is at an earlier stage. It also resembles *Davis* in its voting lineup, except that in *Apple* it was Justice Kavanaugh who joined the four Democratic appointees to form a majority, while Justice Gorsuch voted with the Chief Justice and Justices Thomas and Alito. The federal antitrust statutes are designed to protect consumers and small businesses from companies so dominant that they can drive others out of business and set prices higher than would be possible in a fair market. In this case, consumers accused Apple of using its monopoly over iPhone app sales to force them to pay more than they should for those apps.

The question before the Supreme Court wasn't whether Apple had indeed violated the law, but whether the consumer plaintiffs had the right to bring an antitrust suit against Apple in the first place. In Apple's view, the answer should be no, because the prices the consumers were complaining about were set by the app developers (who pay a 30% commission on each sale to Apple), not by Apple itself. The consumers countered that this was legally irrelevant and that what mattered was who sold them the apps—Apple.

The Justices devoted some space to a debate about precedent but ultimately focused on the practical consequences of the competing approaches. They agreed on the need to find a proper balance between ensuring that injured parties are compensated when a business violates antitrust laws and ensuring that suits by multiple types of plaintiffs don't result in defendants paying more than they really should. (The latter concern is exacerbated by the fact that antitrust statues allow for "treble damages"—awards of three times the actual economic harm suffered.)

Four Justices felt that Apple's was the better approach, but the other five came down on the side of the consumers. This does not mean that Apple will have to pay compensation to these or other consumers or that it will be forced to change its app-selling practices. But it does mean that the case can go forward and that those outcomes remain possible. As for antitrust law more generally, the decision provides some clarification of what relationship between plaintiff and defendant suffices for a lawsuit to be brought. Still, in light of the five-four decision and difficulties in predicting how different rules will play out in practice, it would seem foolish to assume that this is the Court's final word on the subject.

14

Justice Brett Kavanaugh Joins the Court

Lawrence Baum

What the Supreme Court does is largely a product of its membership. For that reason, new appointments to the Court are the subject of widespread interest and heated debate. This is especially true when the departure of a sitting Justice and the arrival of a successor are expected to bring about a substantial shift in the Court's legal policies.

That expectation accompanied the 2018 appointment of Brett Kavanaugh to succeed the retiring Anthony Kennedy.[1] Indeed, many observers of the Court thought that Kavanaugh's appointment would be one of those instances in which a single change in the Court's membership produces a fundamental change in the Court's policies. That expectation can be understood in the context of the Court's recent history.

---

[1]On Kennedy's legacy, see Chapter 10 of *SCOTUS 2018*, "Justice Anthony Kennedy Retires," by Morgan Marietta.

L. Baum (✉)
Ohio State University, Columbus, OH, USA
e-mail: baum.4@polisci.osu.edu

© The Author(s) 2020
D. Klein and M. Marietta (eds.), *SCOTUS 2019*,
https://doi.org/10.1007/978-3-030-29956-9_14

Except for the year-long period in 2016–2017 when one seat was vacant, the Court has had a conservative majority since 1972. But many conservatives have been disappointed with the Court, because it did not move as sharply to the right as they hoped after Republican presidents appointed all ten new Justices between 1969 and 1992. That unexpected outcome came about because several Republican appointees developed moderate or even liberal records as Justices.

Conservatives' disappointment spurred efforts to ensure that Republican presidents chose strongly conservative Justices, and it also helped mobilize conservatives to support Republican presidential candidates. As a presidential candidate who sought to win the approval of conservative leaders and voters, Donald Trump pledged in 2016 to choose his Supreme Court nominees from a list of conservatives (primarily lower-court judges) that he issued. The Federalist Society—the leading association of conservative lawyers—played a key role in compiling that list and two later versions of it.

Neil Gorsuch's 2017 appointment to the Court pleased conservatives. But because Gorsuch succeeded Antonin Scalia, another strong conservative, his arrival at the Court simply restored the ideological balance that had prevailed since 2006: four liberals, four strong conservatives, and one justice (Anthony Kennedy) who was conservative on most issues but who took moderate to liberal positions on some highly visible issues, especially gay and lesbian rights. From 2010 on, the Court's ideological division fell along party lines: The four liberal Justices had been appointed by Democratic presidents, while the five conservatives were Republican appointees.

Kennedy's retirement in 2018 created the opportunity for President Trump to solidify the Court's conservative majority. His choice of Kavanaugh, a federal court of appeals judge, was widely approved by conservatives. With a small Republican majority in the Senate and an increasingly strong tendency for senators to vote along party lines on confirmation of Supreme Court nominees, Kavanaugh was expected to win confirmation by a narrow margin. Indeed, the Senate vote was 50-48 for confirmation. However, his confirmation was delayed by a special Senate hearing about charges of sexual misconduct and assault when he was a student. But the charges and the hearing had very little effect on senators' confirmation votes.[2] Because of the delay, Kavanaugh missed the cases in which the Court heard oral arguments in the first week of the 2018 term.[3]

Expectations About Justice Kavanaugh

Kavanaugh's placement on the list of possible Trump nominees and his actual selection were strong reasons to expect that he would establish a solidly conservative record as a justice. Determined to avoid any mistakes in the selection of Justices, the conservative lawyers who advised Trump on his nominations exercised great care in gathering and assessing evidence about the policy views of candidates for the Court.

Kavanaugh's biography provided considerable basis for confidence in his conservatism.[4] He served as a law clerk for three federal judges appointed by Republican presidents, including Justice Kennedy. He had been on the staff of independent counsel Kenneth Starr, whose investigation of allegations against President Bill Clinton ultimately led to Clinton's impeachment (followed by his acquittal in the Senate). After working with George W. Bush's legal team to help ensure that Bush won the disputed and critical Florida electoral votes in the 2000 presidential election, Kavanaugh served in the Bush White House for five years, until his 2006 appointment to the federal court of appeals.

The court of appeals for the District of Columbia circuit hears a disproportionate number of cases involving major policy issues, and during his dozen years on that court, Kavanaugh established a conservative record. An unusually large number of his law clerks later served as clerks at the Supreme Court, the great majority working with conservative Justices.

---

[2]On this episode, see Chapter 11 of *SCOTUS 2018*, "The Troubled Confirmation of Justice Brett Kavanaugh," by Julie Novkov.

[3]See Chapter 6 on *Gundy*, which was deeply influenced by Kavanaugh's absence.

[4]See Scott Shane et al., "Trump's Choice: Beltway Insider Born and Bred," *The New York Times*, 15 July 2018.

Kavanaugh was quite active in the Federalist Society over the years. This activity was important to his Supreme Court nomination, because involvement in the Society has become almost a prerequisite for selection to the Court by a Republican president. That involvement provided additional evidence of conservative views on issues that he might address as a Justice.

What a Justice's First Term Tells Us

Any single term of the Supreme Court provides only a limited picture of a Justice's place on the ideological spectrum. The particular mix of cases that the Court hears in a term can skew Justices' votes in a liberal or conservative direction. A Justice's first term can be especially misleading, because the Justice's positions on some issues may not be firmly established. Further, even firmly established views about legal policy sometimes shift during a Justice's tenure on the Court.

Even so, the first term provides meaningful evidence about where a Justice stands. Even by the very imperfect measure of percentages of liberal and conservative votes, most Justices show considerable stability: About two-thirds of the Justices appointed since 1969 have had first-year voting records that were within four percentage points of the records for their careers as a whole.[5] A measure of Justices' ideological positions in civil liberties cases (which takes into account changes in the content of cases over time) also shows a high level of stability.[6] We would expect even greater stability for the Justices appointed in the current era, when presidents and their staffs screen prospective nominees so carefully for ideological reliability. Thus, Kavanaugh's first-term record provides meaningful evidence about his likely course during his tenure on the Court.

---

[5]This percentage is based on analysis of data in the Supreme Court Database, archived at http://scdb.wustl.edu.

[6]Data based on this measure, devised by Michael Bailey, are archived at https://michaelbailey.georgetown.domains/data-page-jop-2013/.

There is one complicating factor specific to Kavanaugh. The strong and bitter tone of his testimony in the second hearing on his confirmation to the Court reinforced some observers' perception of him as a strong partisan whose work as a Justice would reflect his antipathy toward Democrats and liberals. Kavanaugh was disturbed by that perception, and he might have wanted to take a relatively moderate stance during his first term as a means to enhance his reputation.

Justice Kavanaugh's Votes and Opinions

Overall, Justice Kavanaugh's voting record was consistent with expectations. Most important, by conventional definitions of "conservative" and "liberal," Kavanaugh had a distinctly conservative record. In decisions that clearly could be characterized in ideological terms, he cast conservative votes 74% of the time.[7] In contrast, in the cases in which Kavanaugh participated, the Court's four Democrats cast conservative votes 23% of the time (Justices Sotomayor and Ginsburg) or 38% of the time (Justices Kagan and Breyer).

The five Republican Justices divided into two groups, the *strong conservatives* (Chief Justice Roberts and Justices Kavanaugh and Gorsuch, all between 68% and 74% conservative), and the *very strong conservatives* (Justices Alito and Thomas, both at 85%). Thus, in his first term Kavanaugh's record was not as conservative as some observers had anticipated.

The proportion of liberal decisions by the Court as a whole was also higher than might have been expected, 40% overall and 44% in non-unanimous decisions. Many of the liberal victories in cases that divided the Justices resulted from votes by one or two conservative

---

[7]In general, votes for litigants who claim that their civil liberties have been violated are characterized as liberal; votes for businesses in conflicts with consumers, employees, and government regulation are characterized as conservative. Justices' votes were not counted in cases in which the ideological meaning of the competing positions was ambiguous or in cases in which Justice Kavanaugh did not participate, so more than one-third of the Court's decisions were excluded. The census case, *Department of Commerce v. New York* (see Chapter 3), was treated as having two decisions because there were important holdings in both ideological directions.

Justices to join with their four liberal colleagues. Gorsuch cast such votes most visibly, joining with the liberals in four 5-4 decisions. But Kavanaugh crossed ideological lines alongside Roberts in three cases, resulting in 6-3 votes for liberal outcomes. In a fourth case, *Apple, Inc. v. Pepper*, he crossed lines alone.[8] In that case, he wrote the Court's opinion for the four liberals and himself, an opinion that allowed consumers to bring an antitrust lawsuit against Apple based on its operation of the "App Store."

Cases are not equal in importance. Two cases in the 2018 term stood out because of their partisan stakes: one about whether partisan gerrymandering of legislative districts could be challenged under the Constitution and another about whether the Trump administration had acted properly in its effort to add a question about citizenship to the 2020 census. In the gerrymandering case, *Rucho v. Common Cause*, Kavanaugh joined his fellow conservatives in a 5-4 decision that prohibited federal courts from considering claims of partisan gerrymandering under the Constitution.[9] In the census case, *Department of Commerce v. New York*, Chief Justice Roberts' majority opinion reached a mixed result.[10] Kavanaugh and the other three conservative associate Justices dissented from the Court's ruling that blocked inclusion of the citizenship question for the time being, but they joined the part of Roberts' opinion that left open the possibility of using the question in the 2020 census if the Trump administration responded with an adequate justification.

Kavanaugh generally took the conservative side in other important cases, but there were exceptions. For instance, he joined a unanimous decision in *Timbs v. Indiana* that applied the Eighth Amendment's prohibition of excessive fines to state cases.[11] Of the seven non-unanimous decisions in which Kavanaugh cast liberal votes, four came in criminal cases and a fifth arose from a criminal prosecution. However,

---

[8]See Chapter 13.
[9]See Chapter 11.
[10]See Chapter 3.
[11]See Chapter 12.

Kavanaugh's votes in criminal cases placed him in the same grouping with Roberts and Gorsuch as his votes across all cases—somewhat more liberal than Alito and Thomas, distinctly less liberal than the Court's Democratic appointees.

When Justices write majority opinions, the content of those opinions may not fully reflect their personal views about a case. To a considerable degree, the same is true of the dissenting opinion assigned by the senior Justice among the dissenters. Other dissenting opinions and concurring opinions, which might be called discretionary, provide more information about the thinking of Justices who write them. The same is true of opinions written by individual Justices at preliminary stages of cases, when the Court decides whether to hear a case or how to respond to a request to issue or dissolve a "stay" of an action by a lower court or another government body.

Kavanaugh wrote discretionary opinions in six cases that the Court decided on the merits. In another three cases, he wrote opinions on stay requests and denials of hearings. One of his discretionary opinions at the merits stage was his concurrence in *Kisor v. Wilkie* (see Chapter 8). That opinion supported limiting judicial deference to interpretations of the law by administrative agencies, an important element of the current conservative legal agenda.

In *American Legion v. American Humanist Association*, the case involving display of a cross on public land, Kavanaugh wrote a concurring opinion that interpreted the Constitution's prohibition of an establishment of religion to allow government support for religion in a wide range of circumstances.[12] This is another element of the conservative legal agenda. Although freedom of religion is an issue that cuts across ideological lines, today conservatives give it particular emphasis on matters such as government aid to religious institutions and exemptions of religious individuals and institutions from certain laws. Two of Kavanaugh's opinions at preliminary stages supported broad interpretations of religious freedom.[13]

---

[12]See Chapter 2.

[13]The cases were *Murphy v. Collier* and *Morris County Board v. Freedom from Religion Foundation*.

In *June Medical Services v. Gee*, Kavanaugh wrote an opinion dissenting from a stay order that prevented a new Louisiana requirement for doctors who perform abortions from going into effect. Speaking for Alito, Thomas, and Gorsuch, he argued that it was too early to conclude that the requirement would create an "undue burden" on women who seek abortions (the standard established in the *Casey* decision in 1992).[14] Although the issue was a narrow one, Kavanaugh's disagreement with Chief Justice Roberts and the Court's liberals suggested something about his views on regulations of abortion.

Aside from specific legal policies, there has been strong support among conservatives in the Federalist Society and elsewhere for two modes of legal interpretation. The first is *textualism* (which rules out efforts to ascertain the intent of lawmakers, instead relying on the specific language of laws). The second is *originalism* (which emphasizes the meaning of the language of laws at the time they were adopted).

Justice Kavanaugh is widely perceived as a textualist and originalist. His first-term opinions provide only limited evidence about his modes of interpretation, but his opinions are generally consistent with those perceptions. In *Rimini Street v. Oracle USA*, for instance, he invoked definitions of a word in early nineteenth-century dictionaries in interpreting an 1831 statute. He seemed to give more weight to precedent than some of his conservative colleagues, though he did join them in two 5-4 decisions that overruled Supreme Court precedents.[15]

Justice Kavanaugh as Speaker and Writer

As a group, the Justices are very active participants in oral argument. Justice Kavanaugh's level of participation did not make him one of the most or least active members of the Court. Not surprisingly for a new

---

[14]*Planned Parenthood v. Casey*, 505 U.S. 833 (1992).
[15]*Franchise Tax Board v. Hyatt* and *Knick v. Township of Scott*.

Justice, his level of participation in arguments increased somewhat over the term.[16]

Kavanaugh wrote seven majority opinions for the Court, seven concurrences and dissents in the Court's full decisions on the merits, and three opinions at the preliminary stages of cases. He wrote in a clear and straightforward style, and his language was sometimes colloquial. He was typically thorough in responding to arguments against the position he took. On the whole, his style of writing was not distinctive. However, when referring to a federal statute he regularly mentioned the name of the president who signed the statute, perhaps as a result of his own experience working with a president.

Justices sometimes adopt a sharp tone in oral argument, berating the lawyers who appear before them. In concurring and dissenting opinions, they sometimes attack colleagues' opinions in sharp terms. Kavanaugh generally avoided those practices. Justices frequently interrupt lawyers and each other; Kavanaugh sometimes apologized for interruptions, and he was relatively deferential to his colleagues. Even when his dissenting opinions expressed strong disagreement with the Court's decision, he was gentler in his criticisms than some other Justices have been. In one of the dissents with strong disagreement, *United States v. Davis*, he carefully emphasized his respect for the majority's position. However, he did join Justice Thomas' very sharply written opinion in the census case.

Summing Up and Looking Ahead

To no one's surprise, Brett Kavanaugh's first-term record was a decidedly conservative one. On one major issue, gerrymandering, his presence on the Court appeared to make a decisive difference: Justice Kennedy was open to the possibility that federal courts could address constitutional

---

[16]Information on oral argument participation is from Tonja Jacobi and Matthew Sage, "October 2018 Term in Review Part I," *SCOTUS OA*, 2 May 2019, scotusoa.com/2018term, and Adam Feldman, "Final Stat Pack for October Term 2018," SCOTUSblog 28 June 2019.

challenges to partisan gerrymandering, but Kavanaugh joined his four conservative colleagues in ruling out that possibility. Yet he stood with John Roberts and Neil Gorsuch as strong conservatives who nonetheless took liberal positions more than a quarter of the time, in contrast with the more consistently conservative Clarence Thomas and Samuel Alito.

A single term provides only a partial picture of what a Justice will be like across a full career, including the positions that the Justice takes on the array of issues of legal policy that the Supreme Court addresses. While it seems certain that Justice Kavanaugh will maintain a conservative record of votes and opinions, it is uncertain just how conservative that record will be. The Court's next term will tell us a good deal more about where Kavanaugh stands, especially because that term will begin with a substantial number of cases on consequential and controversial issues already on the Court's agenda. But it will take considerably longer to learn whether his membership on the Court has the decisive effect on legal policy that was widely anticipated when he was appointed.

Index

CPSIA information can be obtained
at www.ICGtesting.com
Printed in the USA
LVHW031505060220
646085LV00003B/470

9 783030 299552